Tools & Talk

DATA,

CONVERSATION,

AND ACTION

FOR CLASSROOM

AND SCHOOL

IMPROVEMENT

By Michael Murphy

Tools & Talk: Data, Conversation, and Action
for Classroom and School Improvement

By Michael Murphy

Editor: Valerie von Frank
Copy editor: Sue Chevalier
Designer: Kitty Black

Printed in the United States
of America
Item B425
ISBN: 978-0-9800393-7-5

MICHAEL
MURPHY

T
O
O
L S
& T
A L
K

Acknowledgments   5

Foreword   7

Introduction   9

Chapter 1 **A pathway to improvement**   12

Chapter 2 **Tool know-hows**   22

THE TOOLS

Chapter 3 **The Classroom Snapshot Tool and Exchange**   32

Chapter 4 **The Engagement Visit Tool and Exchange**   52

Chapter 5 **The Instructional Design Tool and Exchange**   70

Chapter 6 **The Responsive School Scan Tool and Exchange**   84

Chapter 7 **The Instructional Management Tool and Exchange**   106

Chapter 8 **The missing link:** Building schoolwide analysis   124
           from individual improvement

References   137

About the author   139

Acknowledgments

This work is the result of years of practice in varieties of schools and settings. It represents the synthesis of my beliefs and the evolution of my thinking over the years. The changes in me are a result of influential people who have sparked, nurtured, confounded, challenged, and ultimately shaped me into a better educator.

First, I am extremely grateful to my colleagues at the Institute for Excellence in Urban Education, a program of the Salesmanship Club Youth and Family Centers of Dallas, Texas. Two of the book's tools are a demonstration of collaborative work at the institute. Those at the Salesmanship Club Youth and Family Centers and in the Institute are highly skilled, innovative, and dedicated to results. I am changed because of my work there and the friendships I have formed. While all of my colleagues there have molded my thinking, I thank Kent Skipper, chief executive officer, Delane Kinney, executive director, and my partners there: Paige Conley, Karen Norris, Erica Reyes, Holly Torres, Ann Minnett, Trina Taylor, Sandy Nobles, and Heather Bryant.

In addition, I am indebted to colleagues who have piloted these tools in their schools, including the J. Erik Jonsson Community School (Dallas, Texas), Lee Elementary (Denton Independent School District, Denton, Texas), San Jacinto Elementary (Dallas Independent School District, Dallas, Texas), Elsie Robertson Middle School (Lancaster Independent School District, Lancaster, Texas), Withers Elementary (Dallas Independent School District, Dallas, Texas), Cuellar Elementary (Dallas Independent School District, Dallas, Texas), and all of the elementary and secondary schools in the Greeneville City (Tenn.) Schools. Their enthusiasm and practice with the tools has been immeasurably helpful.

I am also at this point in my life because of the influences of a handful of people who are either my close colleagues and friends and/or admired authors. They include Stephanie Hirsh, Joellen Killion, Rick DuFour, Rebecca DuFour, Jay McTighe, Michael Fullan, Carol Ann Tomlinson, Carlene Murphy, Shirley Hord, Kathryn Kee, Karen Anderson, Sonia Caus Gleason, Cheryl Williams, Betty Ann Fults, Glenn Singleton, and Rick Smith.

Most importantly, I thank my family. My evolution has been nurtured and sparked by my wonderful wife, Debby, an accomplished author and consultant; and my two children, Megan Murphy Hogue and Kevin Murphy, amazing, complex, and accomplished individuals. My family's support and belief in me sustains my desire to make them proud.

— *Michael Murphy*

Foreword

Six decades ago, Edward Deming, a noted statistician, committed to helping post-World War II Japan recover. In his work in Japan and the U.S., he leaned on several core principles to guide business and industry — principles still applied today. In the '80s, Deming's work began a new dawn in education with the introduction of total quality and applied data use in schools.

Educators were not new to data. While Deming was transforming the auto industry, schools had nationally normed achievement test scores that were sent home to parents and neatly stapled into cumulative folders in the school office with students' names printed on them. Parents tried to make sense of the numbers and misinterpreted them. Educators carefully filed those folders and waited to add the next set of test scores.

Fast-forward to today. Data are everywhere. Among NSDC's Standards for Staff Development is one devoted to data: Staff development that improves the learning of all students uses disaggregated student data to determine adult learning priorities, monitor progress, and help sustain continuous improvement. The No Child Left Behind Act calls for states to develop comprehensive data warehouses to make student learning data easily accessible and available to classroom teachers for data-driven instruction. Guidelines for federal stimulus funds and innovation grants call for extensive use of data to improve schools. Federal, state, and local policy call for the use of data to:

- Assess school and district effectiveness;
- Identify student learning needs and intervene to address those needs;
- Identify district, school, and individual teacher goals;
- Rank students, teachers, schools, districts, and states;
- Close schools and send students to others;
- Plan school and district improvements; and
- Measure the achievement of goals.

The national Data Quality Campaign was formed to "expand the ability of state longitudinal data systems to link across the P-20 education pipeline and across state agencies and ensure that data can be accessed, analyzed, and used, and communicate data to all stakeholders to promote continuous improvement" (Data Quality Campaign, 2009).

Yet despite substantial and successful national, state, and district initiatives to make data available to improve student learning, educators are not yet sufficiently using data in the one place where data can make the greatest difference in student learning — the classroom. *Tools & Talk* changes that.

Author Michael Murphy presents a practical and resourceful guide to data use focused on teaching and student learning. Designed for coaches, school administrators, or teams facilitated by teacher leaders, *Tools & Talk* puts resources at the fingertips of those who can benefit most from easy access to and skillful use of data. Written in a no-nonsense, down-to-earth manner with useful tools that can be immediately applied, *Tools & Talk* is accessible for those who fear data, as well as those who love the intricacies of analysis. The tools help frame dialogue with individual teachers and build the relationships necessary to create long-lasting change. Their integrated use in an overall cycle of school improvement bears invaluable promise for school-based specialists and school leaders.

Murphy understands the importance of guiding data users through efficient and effective conversations based on proven protocols and is guided by the clear intent to mine data and relationships to improve teaching and student learning.

Schools and districts ready to amp up their use of data and leverage data analysis as fundamental to the continuous improvement cycle will quickly use this resource in all the best ways and be deeply appreciative to Murphy for making their work more targeted, productive, and effective.

— Joellen Killion
Deputy executive director
National Staff Development Council

Introduction

This book is meant to ignite conversations among colleagues about classroom practices that lead to school improvement and greater student achievement. These conversations will center on change, a difficult process for most who undertake it, and more difficult for those leading change.

Michael Fullan (2001) reminds us that to lead a culture of change, leaders must understand that improvement occurs only when they pay attention to relationships (p. 5). He suggests that if leaders commit themselves to "constantly generating and increasing knowledge inside and outside of the organization," those within that organization will embrace a moral commitment to change and practice change behaviors (p. 6).

The challenge, then, is to align our efforts with these beliefs and to create new ways to honor and nurture educators while softly but persistently demanding that they develop knowledge about practices that support or discourage student success.

The beliefs, strategies, exchange facilitation protocols, and tools in this book represent the most promising of what we know about honoring relationships among educators, focusing on results, and sparking ongoing curiosity about classroom practice and how classroom improvement contributes to overall school improvement.

The strategies, suggestions, protocols, and tools are framed around converging and supportive ideas — building relationships and focusing on collegial, side-by-side dialogue, theory building, and decisions about practice. The five tools, coupled with exchange conversations and aligned with NSDC's Standards for Staff Development, will help teacher leaders, school-based specialists, principals, assistant principals, or academic deans find coherence with the work of classroom coaches or specialists and the work of building leaders and school-based advisory or decision-making teams.

The tools generate data that may serve as valuable benchmarks for school leadership teams' consideration and action. School staff can use these data to consider the degree to which their school is improving in overall instructional practice, engagement, instructional design, responsiveness, and classroom management.

Specific suggestions in the chapters for each tool will help instructional specialists frame exchange conversations with teachers and school leadership teams so staff may feel connected to the data the tools generate and will work to develop their own theories of how to improve their practice.

These tools are not meant to be used to evaluate individual teachers or schools. The tools can be effective only through carefully facilitated conversations about the results, reflection on the meaning of the results, and thoughtful deliberation that leads to theory building and actions to improve.

Each core chapter in this book provides a tool to develop strategic exchanges among colleagues that present a pathway to improvement. These chapters begin with an overview of research that supports the fundamental ideas and beliefs and includes specific information about how to use the tool, how the tool relates to the other tools, and coaching tips on how to use the tool and plan the exchange dialogue that follows its implementation. The tools chapters are divided into these sections:

- **A brief, fictional case study** that matches a classroom improvement dilemma to the tool.
- **Insights:** An introduction and contextual information to build the specialist's command of the tool and its purpose.
- **Deciding to use the tool:** Considerations for deciding to use the tool in one's own context.
- **Selecting participants:** How to select students (if appropriate) and the teachers with whom to use the tool.

- **Building trust:** Creating and sustaining the foundational relationships with the participating teachers and, if appropriate, the students who will be observed.
- **Using the tool:** Step-by-step procedures for using the tool and compiling the data.
- **Planning the exchange:** Suggestions for how the specialist can reflect on the data and prepare his or her notes for the exchange visit.
- **Conducting the exchange:** Methods for building the side-by-side exchange of data and subsequent conversation about classroom practices.
- **Developing theories and making commitments:** Suggestions for how the school-based specialist can move the exchange visit conversation from an analysis of data to actionable theories and substance for subsequent visits. What is the final "contract" between the specialist and the participating teacher concerning the teacher's focus and the next classroom visit?
- **Notes for the building leader:** Additional information for the specialist to consider when using the particular tool and suggestions for how to use aggregated data for dialogue, planning, and action.

The work represented in this book provides a rich source of data for dedicated professionals to begin conversations about improving practice. Educators can use these tools to enhance instructional practices that lead to all students experiencing the success they were meant to have.

To secure printer-ready PDFs of the
tools included in this book, visit:

www.nsdc.org/books/toolsandtalk/

Use password: toolsandtalk376

CHAPTER

1

A PATHWAY

TO IMPROVEMENT

Laura Jones had been a middle school social studies teacher with the Lakefield Consolidated School District for eight years when she applied for an instructional specialist job, a nonsupervisory position working with teachers in a cluster of schools to improve their instruction and effect on student performance. She was selected for the job and assumed her role enthusiastically, but soon learned that she would be on her own to determine much of her daily routine. The original job description provided only a few guidelines, and supervision by the district curriculum director was loose. Jones knew she should focus on improving teacher content, skill, and delivery, but she had few tools to help her gather information about classroom performance and learn to initiate and sustain meaningful, focused, data-driven, change-oriented conversations with teachers. One day, in quiet desperation, she wrote in her journal, "Well, I'm excited that I have this job, but what on earth am I supposed to do? Help!"

Laura Jones is not alone. Thousands of Lauras have taken up new posts in public and private school systems, and they seek assistance in developing relationships with teachers and accelerating improvements for student learning.

The Lakewood Consolidated School District is one of many districts to decide in the last few years to invest in school-based instructional specialists, academic or instructional coaches, or school-based curriculum support staff. The lack of uniformity in titles for this position carries over to job roles. Few schools have clearly defined these specialists' responsibilities. Those hired for these positions, however, have several factors in common: Almost all intend to work directly with teachers, to collaborate with school administrators to elevate the quality of classroom instruction, and to connect teachers with ideas and resources that will enhance teacher performance and raise student achievement levels.

School-based specialists often are selected because of their teaching abilities or their desire for a more systemic role in school improvement. These specialists often are thrust into the position with scant understanding of their new responsibilities and little or no professional development to support them. With few tools, they can become confused, disturbed, or both when they meet with teachers' resistance or when their efforts do not reap quick, lasting school results.

In addition, school-based specialists' work is often misaligned with their school administrator's duties. School administrators often are frustrated about how to work with the school-based specialists and are unclear how to design structures to sustain the specialist's work and use the specialist's work in classrooms monitoring school improvement as required by federal, state, or district mandates.

School-based specialists, school leaders, and school leadership teams can use tools and conversations about data to address these issues and contemplate the degree to which their classrooms and their schools are improving in terms of overall instructional practice, student engagement, instructional design, responsiveness, and classroom management.

Fundamental beliefs

The tools, suggestions, and strategies for conversation in this book are supported by a synthesis of seven beliefs about classroom and school improvement, based on the work of Arthur Costa and Robert Garmston (2002); Carolyn Downey, Betty E. Steffy, Fenwick W. English, Larry

7 statements

These seven statements together are powerful guides for school-based specialists', building leaders', and school leadership teams' practices. These beliefs also align with the National Staff Development Council's Standards for Staff Development, measures by which powerful, actionable professional learning plans are evaluated. The table illustrates this alignment.

E. Frase, and William K. Poston Jr. (2004); Richard DuFour and Robert Eaker (1998); Joellen Killion and Cynthia Harrison (2006); National Staff Development Council (2001); Fred Newmann and Associates (1996); Penelope Jo Wald and Michael S. Castleberry (2000):

1. Teachers' instructional practices must focus on student learning and intended results.
2. Collegial, trusting relationships are critical to adult learning and the changes in attitudes and behaviors that can help students achieve at more sustained and deeper levels.
3. Teachers want to improve their practice, are innately curious about their own knowledge and skills, and are willing to talk about what they know and want to learn.
4. Teachers can use information in reflective ways to think about and change their practices or improve their knowledge and skills.
5. Teachers are able to use information to develop their own results-based theories of what will work better for students.
6. Leaders can gather results of instruments and protocols to align professional learning, support, and resources in order to chart school improvement.
7. School improvement or advisory teams can use the re-

BELIEFS ALIGNED WITH NSDC'S STANDARDS FOR STAFF DEVELOPMENT

Belief	Context	Process	Content
1 Teachers' instructional practices must focus on student learning and intended results.	The beliefs align with each of NSDC's 12 context, process, and content standards, as illustrated by the language below from the standards rationales.		
2 Collegial, trusting relationships are critical to adult learning and the changes in attitudes and behaviors that can help students achieve at more sustained and deeper levels.	**Learning Communities:** "A form of professional learning ... for the purposes of learning, joint lesson planning, and problem solving" (NSDC, 2001, p. 8).	**Collaboration:** "Organized groups provide the social interaction that often deepens learning and the interpersonal support and synergy necessary for creatively solving the complex problems of teaching and learning" (NSDC, 2001, p. 26).	
3 Teachers want to improve their practice, are innately curious about their own knowledge and skills, and are willing to talk about what they know and want to learn.		**Collaboration:** "Organized groups provide the social interaction that often deepens learning and the interpersonal support and synergy necessary for creatively solving the complex problems of teaching and learning" (NSDC, 2001, p. 26).	**Quality Teaching:** "Teachers participate in sustained, intellectually rigorous professional learning regarding the subjects they teach, the strategies they use to teach those subjects ..." (NSDC, 2001, p. 32).
4 Teachers can use information in reflective ways to think about and change their practices or improve their knowledge and skills.		**Data-Driven:** "Because improvements in student learning are a powerful motivator for teachers, evidence of such improvements ... helps sustain teacher momentum during the inevitable frustrations and setbacks that accompany complex change efforts" (NSDC, 2001, p. 16).	**Quality Teaching:** "... engaging in frequent conversations with teachers individually and collectively about instruction and student learning" (NSDC, 2001, p. 32).

Belief	Context	Process	Content
5 Teachers are able to use information to develop their own results-based theories of what will work better for students.		**Research-based:** "It is important that [teachers] design pilot studies to determine the effectiveness of new approaches before proceeding with large-scale implementation" (NSDC, 2001, p. 20).	
6 Leaders can gather results of instruments and protocols to align professional learning, support, and resources in order to chart school improvement.		**Evaluation:** "Evaluation must focus on teachers' acquisition of new knowledge and skills, how that learning affects teaching, and in turn how those changes in practice affect student learning" (NSDC, 2001, p. 18).	
7 School improvement or advisory teams can use the results of instruments and protocols to plan, manage, and accelerate classroom quality.	**Leadership:** "Instructional leaders artfully combine pressure and support to achieve school and district goals" (NSDC, 2001, p. 10).		

sults of instruments and protocols to plan, manage, and accelerate classroom quality.

Change, souls, and promises

Central to all of these beliefs is the idea that real, lasting change results from a combination of reflective data tools, an ensuing exchange dialogue, and development of a meaningful, supportive web of results-focused relationships.

Change is personal. Gene Hall and Shirley Hord (2001) state that the success of any change effort depends not only on what change facilitators (the school-based specialist and building leaders) do, but also on how partic-

ipants individually and collectively interpret and understand their efforts and results (p. 187). In this relationship-based interpretation of change, Hall and Hord state that "all participants in a change process are looking for ways to explain and simplify what is happening" (p. 187).

The success of these tools, then, depends on thoughtful deliberation of what the data mean, and both the specialist and teacher must personally own that deliberation. When supporting staff and teachers understand this approach, they are able to enter into collegial conversations that build trust and propel participants to action. Instead of approaching change with the idea that the school-based specialist has the answers and is seeking ways to share these answers with teachers, the teacher and specialist enter into the change relationship as equals, embarking on a thoughtful analysis of practice, theory building, and action. Participants demonstrate genuine value for, trust in, and a steadfast hold on the value of people, relationships, and collegiality.

In reality, too many teachers perceive a side-by-side conversation with a school-based specialist as risky, assuming the specialist has a preconceived "suggestion" he or she is just waiting to offer.

These "suggestions" actually are thinly masked demands, made in the name of accountability. In many schools, the emphasis on accountability has been translated into the idea that staff need to be held accountable for change, that change should be supported by best practice, and that someone knows what that best practice looks like and should share it with the teacher. This approach implies that a teacher is an empty vessel to whom knowledge must be imparted. In most adults, attempts to force change by dictating the manner in which it occurs will trigger only short-lived improvements. When the school-based specialist or other "expert" is the only one who owns the learning, the teacher may feel forced into change to prevent a negative response but may not cognitively make the change. If, however, school-based specialists embrace a philosophy that all professionals inherently wish to do good work and improve, then participants see the improvement as all-encompassing — accountability-focused, community building, action-oriented, and relationship-focused.

What is needed is change equality. In their book, *The Soul at Work,* Roger Lewin and Birate Regine (1999, p. 333), describe a different way of working for this change equality, in a "genuine relationship based on authenticity and care." When souls are at work, the individual wants to be part of the organization and feels that he or she is contributing to others in a web of connected daily relationships. The tools and exchange conferences are change processes built on this authenticity and care, providing catalysts for relationship-rich, change-focused personal work.

Three ideas are the foundation of the tools and their use:

- Instructional coaches or school-based specialists can enhance their work with classroom teachers by using simple, data-gathering protocols or instruments.

- When teachers and specialists share data from tools in side-by-side exchanges, teachers commit to change their instructional practice.

- Coaches and specialists may aggregate the data gathered through the instruments or protocols into useful, diagnostic summaries that school leadership and site-based advisory teams can use to focus professional learning and resources and to accelerate the improvement process.

The leader's role

The tools and ensuing exchange dialogues in this book provide the foundation and impetus for change and improvement at the classroom and school levels by coupling attention to "souls at work" with relying on impartial, solid data.

School-based specialists, building leaders, and school leadership teams learn to effectively collect classroom data, to talk about the information, and to use the data to address school issues. Building leaders often focus on terminal data, such as state- or nationally normed test scores, and overlook opportunities to use data the instructional specialist may have collected from individual classrooms. These data can provide manageable, interesting, provocative information for school advisory teams to consider and use to formulate and evaluate schoolwide plans for improvement.

School leaders and leadership teams then can create a schoolwide understanding of how individuals' improvements connect to the larger web of school improvement.

CONSTRUCTING BRIDGES

The tools in this book help forge information bridges — connecting classroom improvements and overall school progress. Three fundamental ideas form the progressive piers for this information bridge and coalesce the practices. The three piers guide school-based specialists and school leaders as they collaboratively nurture change. Each pier has practical implications for specialists and building leaders, who work together to align their efforts around these ideas.

First supporting pier

Instructional coaches or school-based specialists can enhance their work with classroom teachers by using simple, data-gathering protocols or instruments.

Contrary to the common assumption that data may be unsettling or unnerving to educators, data compiled into useful information for teachers can provide clarity, be a catalyst for change, and spur institutionalization of the change if educators see evidence of positive student results.

The rationale for NSDC's Data-Driven standard states that "because improvements in student learning are a powerful motivator for teachers, evidence of such improvements … helps sustain teacher momentum during the inevitable frustrations and setbacks that accompany complex change efforts" (NSDC, 2001).

Garmston and Wellman (1999) state, "Productive (group) work is driven by data, both qualitative and quantitative" (p. 44), adding that "collaborative work in schools requires data as well as impressions. In fact, important learnings are possible when the data does and does not align with the impressions of group members" (p. 43).

Specialists can prime teachers to think more deeply and to probe the paradox between the teacher's perception of quality and the results of his or her design or actions by creating data pictures. Data pictures form the basis for "vi-

Practices that support change

The diagram shows how leader practices support classroom or school reflection, analysis, and change. These practices are listed on the central arrow of the diagram and include:

- Relationships and the desire to improve;
- Ongoing inquiry, actions, and knowledge of results;
- Thoughtful deliberation, theory, and action;
- Creation of data pictures;
- Tools to capture information.

These practices support the work and conversation at any level of school change — classroom or system — and are the foundational behaviors through which teachers and leaders can examine improvement. School leaders, the leadership team, and school-based specialists use these practices to align classroom improvement with school improvement and use the tools as information bridges from classroom to school level. The diagram shows how these practices help transfer information from the classroom level and translate data into larger data pictures that school leaders and leadership teams use to review, reflect, and deliberate on as they seek ways to determine whether their systemic efforts are making a difference.

sual dialogue" (Easton, 2008), which triggers an emotional and cognitive response to the observed teacher's behaviors and resultant student responses. Visual dialogue connects what teachers see and what they hear during col-

THE INFORMATION BRIDGE PROCESS

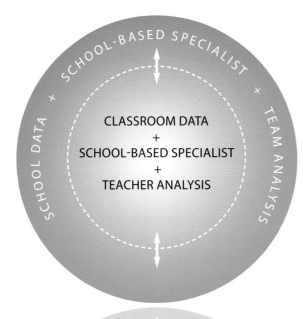

SCHOOL-BASED SPECIALIST

SCHOOL DATA + + TEAM ANALYSIS

CLASSROOM DATA
+
SCHOOL-BASED SPECIALIST
+
TEACHER ANALYSIS

Relationships and the desire to improve

Ongoing inquiry, actions, and knowledge of results

Thoughtful deliberation, theory building, and action

Creation of "data pictures"

Tools to capture information

legial conversations. Each participating teacher receives clear and timely information about his or her results compared with a set of classroom and/or school standards. In shaping data pictures, teachers are able to interpret information so they can understand the complexities of instructional practice and can own the action to create classroom improvements.

Specialists and teachers often do not know how to initiate conversations about practice without a starting device. Downey et al. (2004) detail teachers' hesitation in these data-driven conversations and how best efforts often are met with confusing, unsatisfying outcomes.

Tools, while they enhance the examination of practice through meaningful conversations, are not ends in themselves. Tools combined with a desire for change, supportive conversations, and "data-boosting questions" (Holcomb, 2009, p. 184) can help the teacher and school-based specialist "focus on specific data, while drawing out interpretations and reactions … avoiding them 'telling' what the findings mean or what action should be taken" (p. 185).

Tools can help specialists generate data to create data pictures and initiate a dialogue about classroom practice and potential student results. Coupled with building relationships between the participants, tools can provide structure, boundaries, and a framework for a focused conversation about improvement. Participants find comfort in a clear structure and a road map for thoughtful conversations. The structure and framework of collegial conversations must be part of transforming data into information that leads to classroom changes.

Second supporting pier

When teachers and specialists share data from tools in side-by-side exchanges, teachers commit to change their instructional practice.

"Teachers make meaning based on their lived experiences. Meaning changes as they reflect about experience," according to Downey et al. (2004, p. 135). "The process … is gradual and can be accelerated and supported through dialogue that brings to consciousness deeply held beliefs that often reside at the subconscious level."

Specialists help teachers make meaning of data collected using tools and help them focus and accelerate their learning through deliberate, strategic dialogue between colleagues. Tools yield data for the conversation, and an exchange conference helps the teacher develop his or her own contextually based theory of how changes in practice might result in greater student achievement.

These side-by-side conversational exchanges are effective, beneficial to all participants, and result in change when the teacher and school-based specialist feel that there is a mutual purpose to the work.

Patterson, Grenny, McMillan, and Switzler (2002, p. 69) call this mutual purpose the idea that "we are working toward a common outcome in the conversation, that we care about (their) goals, interests, and values."

Teachers sometimes are reluctant to participate in such data-filled exchanges, not because they do not want to discuss instruction, but often because they have not experienced the kind of conversation that reveals practices and underlying beliefs and actions around classroom practice.

Downey et al. (2004, p. 136) state that "the majority of teachers working in classrooms today do not have the skills necessary to question their behavior, reflect about practice, seek out new knowledge and change their practice so that more children are learning at high levels."

To reach the goal of changed practice, specialists support and prime the teacher, developing dialogue skills and helping the teacher reach what Lev Vygotsky (1978) termed the "zone of proximal development," which results in effective dialogue and discussion that lead to individual growth.

The rationale for NSDC's Collaboration standard states that learning is a social endeavor, and that interpersonal support and momentum can improve teaching and learning (NSDC, 2001). When teachers and specialists forge strong relationships that allow them to engage in side-by-side, focused dialogue around data, teachers will build new theories and modify their practices to make their instruction more effective for students.

Changes that result from single efforts may be profound for teachers and students, but data on the collective changes will provide school leaders and leadership teams with periodic checks about whether their sustained actions are yielding schoolwide progress toward systemic and lasting gains.

Third supporting pier

Coaches and specialists may aggregate the data gathered through the instruments or protocols into useful, diagnostic summaries that school leadership and site-based advisory teams can use to focus professional learning and resources and to accelerate the improvement process.

Collecting and using classroom data as a catalyst for thoughtful deliberation between two colleagues is powerful learning in itself. However, work with individual teachers may result in only individual pockets of success. When school leaders make a strategic determination to look simultaneously at classroom and school improvement using aggregated classroom data, the leadership team can use the data to support individual teacher accomplishment and to create organizational knowledge, keys to school improvement.

Organizational knowledge creation is defined by Nonaka and Takeuchi (1995, p. 3) as the "capability of a company (or a school) to create new knowledge, disseminate it throughout the organization, and embody it in products, services, and systems."

Linking classroom analysis and school improvement takes effort and careful planning. School leadership team members have to have open conversations linking individual decision making and practice with the school's improvement effort.

Tools alone are not the mechanism for creating knowledge. The tools yield the data on which school leaders deliberate and then use to develop ideas to improve teacher and student learning.

The school leader facilitates thinking that starts with explicit knowledge but uses it only to launch the development of tacit knowledge, which is highly personal, hard to formalize, and resides at the heart of the school improvement issue. Tacit knowledge is critical for organizations to "shift to a new state as a result of the new interactions and ideas. Such new states represent breakthroughs in which greater coherence is achieved" (Fullan, 2001, pp. 114-115).

The bridge to meaning

Merely using the tools in this book and subsequent exchange conferences, either at the classroom or school level, will not ensure the success of classroom or school-wide change. Before using the tools, leaders must explore how "meaning making" is built and supported. The tools and exchange conferences will not create collegial relationships. The promise of the tools can be realized only if specialists and leaders relentlessly pursue data and believe in teachers' desire to improve their practice to be more successful. The school-based specialist, building leader, and school leadership team must collectively believe that:

- Any improvement conversation and exchange of ideas between two people must be based on a strong, collegial, trusting relationship;

- The focus of any tool, data, and conversation must start from understanding but build toward actions and demonstrable results; and

- Capitalizing on the teacher's curiosity about his or her own practice is central to igniting learning, decisions, and improvement.

The five tools in this series can be used individually or in combination and are not intended to be used in any particular sequence. Some link classroom improvement and school analysis. Others are intended to be used only at the school level. Either way, tools provide the school leadership team with information to link individual accomplishment to school accomplishment and to bridge the two concepts, and help teachers achieve what they naturally want — a sense of personal worth and efficacy, connections to the organization and the people within it, and results.

CHAPTER

T O O L KNOW-HOWS

Before beginning to use the tools, reflect on the intented result — classroom improvement, school improvement, or both — and clarify expected outcomes to create a sound process built on fundamental relationships, respect, and exchanges. Reviewing several cautions before beginning the tools and exchange conferences will help users become aware of potential issues along the way.

1. Know your stuff.

Educators in various roles can use these tools to accomplish various goals. School-based specialists might use them to support individual work with teachers at one school or multiple sites. Building leaders might use the tools to create data-supported, results-based conversations with teachers in lieu of traditional evaluative conferences or walk-throughs. Either school-based specialists or building leaders might aggregate the data from the tools to stimulate discussions with school improvement teams about the quality of education at the school and progress toward goals. District leaders might use any or all the tools to get a sense of district quality or how well teachers districtwide are attaining standards of practice.

In all cases, study the tools before using them and learn how to complete them and how to derive meaning from the resulting data. Practice completing samples of any or all of the tools in controlled settings with a colleague or groups of teachers who understand that data gathering is a practice before implementation.

Preparation cannot be overvalued; indeed, it is crucial to the efficacy of any of the tools and exchange conferences. The specialist or leader must be able to visit the classroom quickly and complete a tool within minutes. Several tools include interrelated factors, so being familiar with the tool will allow the user to know when simultaneous factors are being observed and to accurately mark the tool.

In addition to understanding the tools, understand why a particular tool is useful. Participating teachers may ask for definitions for the tool's indicators. Become familiar with the details of each tool so that these initial conversations with teachers build the confidence and mutual interdependence vital to reflection and improvement.

Finally, be clear about the expected outcome for the exchange conference and carefully plan conversation markers to use during the conference. Study the data from the tool to prepare for that collegial conversation with the teacher. Remember that the goal of the exchange conference is mutual understanding and agreed-upon action. Careful data analysis and planning before the exchange conversation lead to the most meaningful dialogue and action. Each chapter includes facilitation prompts to guide users in planning and conducting the exchange conference.

To prepare for the exchange conference:

1. Review the selected tool and the data.

2. Reflect on the tool's purpose and why it could be helpful for this teacher.

3. Scan the data and jot down two or three overall impressions that the data reveal. ("What, in general, did I see?")

4. Reflect on the exchange conference facilitation prompts at the end of each chapter.

5. Briefly list conversation markers to follow during the exchange conference.

6. Mentally rehearse the beginning of the exchange conference, thinking through how to start the conversation.

Despite the best planning, conversations often take

Getting inside the tools

The tool use chart shows the Classroom Snapshot Tool's seven broad categories and which other tools are primarily aligned with each category. The relationship among the tools is laid out for specialists and leaders to select the appropriate tool.

For example, if the snapshot revealed a general concern in multiple classrooms about classroom instructional design, the specialist or building leader might use the Instructional Design Tool, the Responsive School Scan Tool, or the Instructional Management Tool to drill down into the nature of the issue and explore possible remedies. The tools are not meant to be used sequentially. School leaders and specialists must consider which tool serves their purpose.

Some of the tools are intended to be used in individual classrooms and to allow the specialist or school leader to collect individual data to analyze and discuss with the participating teacher. The Classroom Snapshot Tool and the Responsive School Scan Tool are intended to be used in multiple classrooms or throughout the school to capture how teachers are performing related to the standards in each tool at a specific moment in time.

detours, and a thoughtful plan may have to be abandoned because of questions and conversation. Preparing broad markers and leading questions, however, not only provides

TOOL USE CHART

Classroom Snapshot Tool concerns	Engagement Visit Tool Chapter 4	Instructional Design Tool Chapter 5	Responsive School Scan Tool Chapter 6	Instructional Management Tool Chapter 7
RESPONSIVE, BRAIN-BASED CLASSROOMS				
Classroom instructional design		✓	✓	✓
Teacher instructional strategies		✓		
Student responsiveness	✓			✓
ENGAGING STUDENT TASKS				
Content design		✓		✓
Content delivery	✓		✓	
COMMUNITY OF RESPECT AND LEARNING				
Cultural responsiveness	✓		✓	✓
Classroom standards		✓	✓	✓

structure, but also establishes a logical, reassuring level of comfort for the participating teacher that leads to greater trust.

2. Know how the tools interrelate.

The tools share a common philosophy, indicators, and strands, connections that can initially be seen through the Classroom Snapshot Tool. As school-based specialists or leaders learn and use different tools, they will see some indicators appear in more than one tool. One diagnostic and/or benchmark tool that examines many dimensions of classroom quality is the Classroom Snapshot Tool. This tool, explained in Chapter 3, may be used to accumulate snapshots of overall classroom quality and point to a need to use additional, more focused, tools. The Classroom Snapshot Tool includes 27 indicators, data from which can be aggregated for multiple classrooms to form a picture of a school on a particular day. Ten to 15 of the Classroom Snapshot Tool indicators are found in at least one other tool. Because the snapshot is the broadest overview of instructional quality, its results may lead to additional questions or analysis and into other tools to provide specific support. These relationships are intentional to help users by providing flexibility in matching the appropriate tool to a goal or a need the teacher expresses.

3. Know your role.

In a conventional working relationship with a teacher, the specialist or school leader assumes a consulting role and shares his or her expertise with the teacher. In these tool exchange conferences, however, the goal is to share data and have a side-by-side conversation. The specialist or school leader takes more of a coaching, collegial role and allows the teacher the prominent role in the exchange, wondering aloud about what the data show concerning the teacher's practice and speculating about what might make instruction more effective. The specialist or school leader facilitates the teacher's thinking and listens to what the teacher believes will enhance his or her practice. The specialist or building leader does not manipulate the teacher

Case study

A fictional case study shows how one school-based specialist decided on additional tool(s) to use after the initial Classroom Snapshot Tool.

into a predetermined decision, but primes the teacher's thinking and helps ensure the result of the conversation is greater insight and, most importantly, action. The specialist or school leader prepares only broad benchmarks for conversation — questions or reflections to assist and support the teacher as he or she decides on future actions.

The role of collegial coach is difficult for most current school-based specialists and school leaders, who likely have been hired to their post because they have curricular or instructional expertise. It is hard not to share the expertise that they have developed. Many school districts include consulting with teachers in the school-based specialist's job description; however, acting as the expert will limit change because the specialist will own the learning rather than the teacher. Teachers traditionally have been told what to do to improve, not required to take charge of their own improvement.

School leaders also have role dilemmas, feeling the urgent need for classroom and school improvement propelling them into looking for short-term gains rather than collaborative adult learning practices that could be most effective. The tools and exchange conferences require leaders to deliberate over data and facilitate teacher decisions. The principal is not expected to appear in the classroom, gather data, and then suggest improvements to the teacher. The principal's role is to gather data and work with the teacher to facilitate the teacher's thinking — just as the effective specialist facilitates the teacher's thinking and an effective teacher facilitates student learning.

MIDDLE SCHOOL DESIGN

Saano Murembya, the school-based specialist at Macomb Middle School, gets support from his principal and the school improvement team to use the Classroom Snapshot Tool to get a sense of overall classroom quality. He observes 14 classrooms one morning, 35% of the teachers at Macomb. Analyzing the aggregated data, Murembya notices a pattern — many of the "no" indicators are in the classroom instructional design category. The snapshot indicates an absence of:

- Varieties of visible print and student work;
- Physical grouping areas and open space;
- An attractive, rich learning environment; and
- Effective pacing of instructional time.

Murembya wants more information and decides to look for another tool to get more specific data about classroom instructional design. He finds three tools relate to this category — the Instructional Design Tool, the Responsive School Scan Tool, and the Instructional Management Tool (see Tool Use Chart, p. 25). He then must pick the tool or tools to match the school's issue within classroom instructional design. For instance, if the issue really is efficient pacing of instructional time, Murembya may use the Instructional Management Tool, which contains a section that tracks instructional transitions during the observed time. If the issue is more about the absence of an attractive, rich environment and the related lack of student voice in the classroom (who are the kids in the classroom, and do you get a sense of them by looking at the learning environment?), Murembya may use the Responsive School Scan Tool. If the underlying issue is the classroom's physical arrangement, he will use the Instructional Design Tool since seven of the indicators in the Instructional Design Tool address ways classroom design supports powerful instruction.

The principal also may share aggregated data from the tools with school improvement teams for planning. If the principal uses the data as a way to measure progress in school improvement, the school improvement team can be an integral part — perhaps for the first time — of examining and analyzing ongoing data.

In this approach, the building leader takes on three new roles: facilitating adult learning through side-by-side exchange conferences; accumulating data to focus on classroom excellence; and leading thinking, analysis, and planning so the school improvement team has the information members need to assess improvement milestones, determine resources and support systems to help teachers improve, and design professional learning that aligns with emerging needs highlighted by data from the tools.

4. Know when to listen.

Data, coupled with thoughtful, deliberate conversation, will build relationships and create action for classroom and school improvement. The school-based specialist or school leader collects data and facilitates reflection and thinking around the data. To effectively facilitate reflection and thinking requires something unheard of in many schools: silence. Listening is the essence of relationship building. Great facilitators of thinking shift ownership of the conversation from the "expert" (the school-based specialist or building leader) to the professionals sitting around the table. One strategy is to offer a conversation starter and then keep quiet. Participants may be confounded at first, but once they realize this is the new process, they will feel compelled to work harder, think more deeply, and offer more ideas. The school-based specialist or school leader will learn more, as well. Rather than planning what to say next, he or she will be listening for nuances of the other person's learning. All participants gain from listening more to each other and will find that they learn a great deal from the expertise around the table.

To create a productive learning relationship:

Refrain from making judgments. Observers often make quick assumptions about what they see in classrooms, forming opinions, impressions, interpretations, and evaluations. Judgments create a dangerous inner dialogue that affects our work with others and how we hear them. While it may be impossible to avoid appraising a situation, the key is to develop awareness of one's judgments and how personal opinions filter the information we hear or see.

For example, in Chapter 4, Ben Keller, a congenial 3rd-grade teacher, seeks the school specialist's help to better engage his students. The specialist may be pleased that Keller asks for her help. Prior to observing in Keller's class, she might say, "It's great that Ben wants to improve and is concerned about his class. I can't wait to see how I can help him." The specialist has decided that Keller will be a willing participant in this relationship, and her appraisal may filter her attitudes and behaviors. Being aware of her feelings will allow the specialist to more accurately capture data when she visits Keller's room and as she facilitates the dialogue with Keller to think about and plan for improvement.

Appraisals can lead to negative interpretations. Suppose the specialist visits Keller's classroom and is disappointed by his teaching skills. Her appraisal may alter her inner dialogue, and her conversation with him could become a one-way list of suggestions for improvement. The purpose of the exchange conference, however, is to achieve a side-by-side dialogue grounded in reflection and action. The specialist needs to be aware of any predispositions toward Keller and his teaching skill as she prepares for and engages in the exchange.

Verbal reflection takes practice

Using verbal reflection strategies requires practice. They are most effective when used sparingly. Most educators can remember feeling twinges of annoyance with a facilitator who used, over and over and over, "I think you are saying …." Using verbal reflection requires carefully listening to the responses, which will either confirm the reflection or adjust it. Either way, the resulting information allows the facilitator to more accurately ascertain what is being deliberated.

Verbal reflection strategies are critical to the success of the exchange conferences, and they are best used when a pause is necessary in the exchange and/or a decision needs to be solidified or a milestone is reached. Plan for those critical strategies, and look for logical places to use them.

Practice verbal reflection. The school-based specialist or school leader facilitates a conversation around the data so that the teacher or teachers feel connected to the data and the learning. Offered respectfully and thoughtfully, these verbal reflection strategies are like trial balloons — permissions for the specialist or the school leader to prime the conversation, ask for elaboration, or make an adjustment.

Verbal reflection strategies attempt to calibrate both the content of the conversation and participants' emotions. The specialist or school leader verbally surfaces ideas or statements in order to sort out personal filters (interpretations, evaluations, or impressions of the data and the emotions of those involved in the exchange) and to align the people, their emotions, and the ideas being discussed. The specialist or leader asks the participant or participants

VERBAL REFLECTION STARTERS

VERBAL REFLECTION STEM	GOAL OF REFLECTION STRATEGY
"It seems that you are saying (asking) . . ."	Paraphrasing
"So it looks like what we have talked about is . . ."	Paraphrasing
"So next time, you will be attempting to . . ."	Paraphrasing
"If you were to boil this down into one statement, what would it be?"	Summarization
"What is this all about?"	Summarization
"Could you help me out with one part of your statement?"	Clarification
"Are you thinking about the effects of . . ."	Clarification
"What you are suggesting is . . ."	Paraphrasing or clarification
"Do you mean that . . ."	Paraphrasing or clarification
"Are you wondering whether . . ."	Paraphrasing or clarification

to reflect on the idea and offers mid-exchange adjustments to ensure that the conversation is clear and moving as intended.

Some common verbal reflection strategies include summarizing, clarifying, and paraphrasing.

- *Summarizing* captures the essence of the conversation with few details but an overall view of what is being said or learned.
- *Clarifying* attempts to get clear on one or more aspects of the conversation or to clear up possible misconceptions.
- *Paraphrasing* repeats the learning or conversation in the user's own words to determine whether there is common understanding.

A final word

The next five chapters detail each tool. Using the tools is hard work and requires intensive preparation. School-based specialists and school leaders should reflect on their own theories of change and how they believe change happens. The tools and exchange conferences will spark dis-

How the tools are connected

The concepts and indicators from the Classroom Snapshot Tool are seen in each of the other tools. Each of the four tools in the lower part of the graphic represent a more narrow focus as suggested by the tool's title. The connecting lines illustrate the relationship among the tools. Focused conversation and planning provide the grounding framework for each tool.

cussions about intent, practice, and action, and drive more profound conversation. Although collegial, collaborative, and relationship-rich, the use of the tools holds teachers, specialist, and school leaders accountable. Using the tools and data, participants are thrust into deliberate, actionable conversations about classroom practice and a focus on the real beneficiaries of the work — the students.

SCHOOL IMPROVEMENT EXCHANGE TOOLS

The Classroom Snapshot Tool and Exchange

| Designing and facilitating responsive brain-based classrooms | Enhancing curriculum to provide engaging student tasks | Creating communities of respect and learning |

The Engagement Visit Tool and Exchange

The Instructional Design Tool and Exchange

The Responsive School Scan Tool and Exchange

The Instructional Management Tool and Exchange

FOCUSED CONVERSATION AND PLANNING /
FOCUSED CONVERSATION AND PLANNING /
FOCUSED CONVERSATION AND PLANNING /
FOCUSED CONVERSATION AND PLANNING /

CHAPTER

The CLASSROOM SNAPSHOT T O O L

& EXCHANGE

Marisol Norales, an instructional specialist, works with teachers at Ledbetter Middle School and has a strong collegial relationship with Ledbetter's principal, Lida Jones. Jones shared her frustrations when speaking with Norales:

"Teachers have been willing to look at their instructional practices, and they've been receptive to professional learning. I feel really good about that. But I know — at least I think I know — that our results are inconsistent. We seem to have pockets of success, but I don't really have any schoolwide evidence of teachers making changes in their instructional planning and delivery.

"And when I meet with my leadership team to talk about how we're doing, I have a hard time finding data to share. The only information I have is from benchmark tests and the state exams, but that information doesn't encourage the staff to continue looking at classroom strategies. I wish we had something that would help us look informally at classroom practices and would be a yardstick to measure progress. How can we capture promising practices we believe are linked to student performance?"

Jones voices common frustrations:

1. How do schools get a picture of overall classroom practices?

2. How can leaders aggregate such information into useful data for teachers and the school's leadership team?

3. How can these data spark schoolwide dialogue about progress and promote ongoing learning and change?

Norales and Jones may begin to address these questions by using the Classroom Snapshot Tool, a checklist of 27 indicators that allows the specialist to quickly gather information in a classroom by filling in the one-page chart of what observers might see in a quality classroom.

THE CLASSROOM SNAPSHOT TOOL

Date and time _____   School _____   Grade _____   Subject _____

Classroom teacher _____   Classroom activity during observation _____

RESPONSIVE, BRAIN-BASED CLASSROOMS	YES	NO
CLASSROOM INSTRUCTIONAL DESIGN		
Varieties of visible print and student work		
Group areas and open space		
Attractive, rich learning environment		
Efficient pacing of instructional time		
TEACHER INSTRUCTIONAL STRATEGIES		
Varieties of materials and resources		
Varieties of teacher-directed strategies		
Assessment incorporated into the teaching segment		
Clear teacher instructional communication and instructional sequencing		
STUDENT RESPONSIVENESS		
Student routines and management of own learning		
Suitable, appropriate student movement		

ENGAGING STUDENT TASKS	YES	NO
CONTENT DESIGN		
Respectful tasks for all students		
Focus on student understanding		
Inquiry- and/or experience-based		
Focus on real-world application		
Differentiation of content, process, and/or product		
CONTENT DELIVERY		
Purposeful student conversation with the teacher		
Evidence of student engagement in task		
Seamless use of materials		
Varieties of instructional groupings		

COMMUNITY OF RESPECT AND LEARNING	YES	NO
CULTURAL RESPONSIVENESS		
Overall culture of fairness and equality		
Respectful teacher directions		
Established and fair student routines		
Teacher capitalization on student interests		
Teacher-student connections		
CLASSROOM STANDARDS		
Visuals indicating class guidelines or desired social behaviors		
Room arrangement to support student and teacher community		
Daily learning goals posted for student and teacher view		

NOTES:

The Institute for Excellence in Urban Education, a program of the Salesmanship Club Youth and Family Centers, contributed to the development of this tool.

▪ INSIGHTS

The Classroom Snapshot Tool evolved from the idea that three key clusters of practices are aligned with student performance. These practices are from research at the J. Erik Jonsson Community School and the Institute for Excellence in Urban Education (both programs of the Dallas, Texas, nonprofit Salesmanship Club Youth and Family Centers). The practices also are supported by research (Gay, 2000; Marzano, 2003b; Newmann, 1996; Tomlinson, 2001). The three clusters create a broad view of classroom quality. The areas and the supporting research for each are:

- **Responsive, brain-based classrooms.** Has the teacher designed the classroom to develop and promote deep learning? Do students have a variety of print materials and resources to use as they learn? Does the teacher clearly vary the strategies that he or she uses, and do students respond effectively and efficiently (Gay, 2000; Glatthorn, Boschee, & Whitehead, 2006; Marzano, 2003b)?

- **Engaging student tasks.** What tasks are students asked to complete, and are all the tasks appropriate to the students' age, ability, and interest? Does the teacher focus on students' understanding, demonstrated by teacher-to-student and student-to-teacher communication and questions? Do instructional groupings help students accomplish assigned tasks (Gay, 2000; Marzano, 2003b; Newmann, 1996; Tomlinson, 2001)?

- **Community of respect and learning.** Does the classroom climate foster student risk taking and communication? Has the teacher set high expectations? Does the interplay between student and teacher and among students promote fairness, interest, collaboration, and community (Gay, 2000; Jensen, 1998; Marzano, 2003a; Tomlinson, 2001)?

The Classroom Snapshot Tool provides a broad view of classroom quality in any school. While the tool helps recorders observe practices in individual classrooms, its power is in a collective, diagnostic summary that allows the leadership team or whole faculty to begin or extend a dialogue about teachers' visions of a high-quality classroom. With multiple observations using the tool, the school leader or the leadership team can see aggregated information and can begin to talk about a snapshot of classroom and overall school quality.

The aggregated data will also ignite a dialogue among school staff about the quality of teaching and learning in the school and teachers' visions for instruction. Many teachers do not have much practice talking about their own craft. Carolyn Downey, in *The Three-Minute Classroom Walk-Through* (Corwin Press, 2004, p. 136), said, "Teachers have difficulty promoting their own growth. Without assistance, a few teachers can promote their own growth and development, but the vast majority of them do not have these skills." Downey said teachers need to exchange ideas in "thoughtful dialogue leading to growth" and that "teachers are naturally curious, especially when it comes to being more effective in the classroom" (pp. 136-137).

The Classroom Snapshot Tool not only provides data but also stimulates data-driven conversations that can lead to school improvement decisions around school quality. By discussing the results of multiple snapshots, staff members begin to consider and take responsibility for the research-based indicators in the tool and can be propelled to commit to a newly focused vision for high-quality classroom instruction.

▪ SELECTING PARTICIPANTS

The Classroom Snapshot Tool is best used to aggregate data from multiple classrooms, so carefully plan the day or days to use the tool. Using a school roster showing grade levels, departments, and individual teacher names, select a random sampling of teachers representative of the entire faculty across grades and subjects. The sample taken on a single day should represent at least 30% of the teaching staff, if at all possible, so that the aggregated data represent a sizeable portion of the faculty. Presenting information to the leadership team about 10 teachers out of 88, for example — 11% of the faculty — will not be as meaningful.

■ DECIDING TO USE THE TOOL

The Classroom Snapshot Tool is a benchmark tool that can be used to examine several dimensions of teachers' design and delivery of instruction. Because the tool paints a broad view of overall learning quality, use the snapshot before using other tools or use the snapshot results to indicate which other tools to use next.

Use the Classroom Snapshot Tool to:

- Collect information about general classroom practices;
- Gather data about one teacher's classroom practices to diagnose areas for future support;
- Look at a school profile of instructional practices by aggregating individual snapshots;
- Provide the school leadership team with formative data that might reflect how school improvement efforts are affecting overall classroom quality; and/or
- Diagnose specific areas for future work and professional learning.

■ BUILDING TRUST

While many teachers are becoming more comfortable with informal walk-throughs, the Classroom Snapshot Tool may generate both curiosity and concern among teachers. The school-based specialist and the leadership team will want to talk with teachers about the purpose for using the snapshot and where the data may lead. School leaders should emphasize to faculty that the tool will not be used as a teacher evaluation but to begin conversations schoolwide about teaching practices. In addition, the specialist will want to communicate to both school leaders and the school leadership team that any individual teacher data will not be disseminated to them for review or evaluation purposes.

Some teachers initially may view the snapshot as a "teaching audit" and fear repercussions or mandated changes. Teachers may need to be assured that 1) individual classroom data will be aggregated into a school profile; 2) the classroom visit will be brief, not more than about 15 minutes; and 3) the specialist will not share an individual teacher's data with school leaders. If, in rare cases, the Classroom Snapshot Tool is used to diagnose individual teacher practices in order to provide support, that teacher must understand that the snapshot is being used only to look at areas of quality and will not be used as formative data for the teacher's evaluation.

Checklist of materials for the Classroom Snapshot Tool

- ☐ One Classroom Snapshot Tool for each classroom
- ☐ Clipboard or hard writing surface
- ☐ Extra pencils or pens
- ☐ Timer or watch
- ☐ School map, roster, and schedules
- ☐ Definitions (optional)

To build trust:

1. The specialist should talk with the school leader and/or leadership team about the purpose of using the tool and what teachers will need to know ahead of the first visits.

2. The specialist should ask the building leader and/or leadership team to talk with teachers and then relate any concerns before the specialist uses the snapshot.

3. Before meeting with the faculty, leaders should decide whether they want a snapshot of what classroom quality is like before teachers know any of the tool's specifics. If so, rather than sharing the tool itself, lead-

ers will want to talk with the faculty about its underlying concepts.

4. If building leaders decide to share all aspects of the Classroom Snapshot Tool with the faculty before using it, they should review the major components of the tool and the operational definitions of the 27 indicators of the tool to ensure understanding.

These faculty meetings can build trust through the transparency of both sharing the tool and discussing the purpose of using it in the school. The leader should explain how the snapshot will be used and how it will provide valuable data about classroom practices. The leader should let teachers know that the specialist generally does not share an individual teacher's results with him or her, but aggregates the results for the school.

Depending on the purpose of the faculty meeting and the amount of intended information to share, ideas for deepening the classroom snapshot discussion are to:

• Break the faculty into groups.

• Assign each group one of the categories of indicators, and have members brainstorm what that idea would look like in the classroom using table sticky notes or chart paper.

• Display the tables' work and discuss.

• Share the actual operational definitions of the snapshot.
   Or

• Post several large pieces of chart paper on the walls, each with a header of one of the snapshot's subcategories: classroom instructional design, teacher instructional practices, student responsiveness, content design, content delivery, cultural responsiveness, and classroom standards.

• Engage the faculty in a carousel brainstorming session in which the faculty members split into smaller groups, each group starting at one of the seven posted charts and brainstorming what that concept would look like in practice at their school. After a short period for brainstorming and posting ideas, the facilitator calls time and the groups move clockwise, adding to posted lists. The process continues until each group has moved around to all seven charts.

• Share promising research that supports the tool's indicators (Gay, 2000; Marzano, 2003b; Newmann, 1996; Tomlinson, 2001).

• Share the operational definitions.

• Debrief and discuss.

Before the day of the snapshot, the specialist and school leader should make sure their preparation has addressed these questions:

• What has been done to ensure that teachers are accepting of the specialist's classroom visits?

• Has the principal or the leadership team shared a blank Classroom Snapshot Tool with the teachers and discussed the indicators?

• Has the leadership team endorsed the use of the snapshot?

• Are members of the leadership team prepared to answer questions about the snapshot and why they support its use?

• Do teachers know which day the specialist will use the tool?

• What plans are in place to engage the teachers and the leadership team in a dialogue around the results?

• What preliminary plans are in place to use the aggregated data to propel either school improvement planning or professional learning planning?

■ USING THE TOOL

- **Plan the classroom snapshot observation day** by first accessing individual teacher schedules to ensure that the intended instruction in the scheduled subject is observed. Completing 12 to 15 snapshots generally takes about three hours.

- **Briefly greet the teacher** at the beginning and thank the teacher at the conclusion of the observation, if the moment is appropriate. Try to be as unobtrusive as possible. However, depending on the classroom and the nature of the instruction, it may be important to walk around to find evidence of the indicators.

- **Note the start time** and keep an eye on the timer or clock to limit the visit to between 12 minutes and 15 minutes, and record the practices described in each snapshot indicator. Many of the 27 indicators are static "look fors" that can simply be checked off when found. The majority, however, may require observing for the entire visit and weighing the teacher's overall use of that practice before tallying "yes" or "no." A notes section at the end of the grid allows for noting any questions or overall impressions.

- **Look over the tool** to make sure all indicators are marked, the time is noted, and then prepare another tool form for the next classroom. Continue until all of the individual classroom snapshots are completed for the selected number of teachers that day.

Practice the indicators

The Classroom Snapshot Tool is a checklist. The specialist drops in to selected classrooms to complete the tool during 12 minutes to 15 minutes of continuous observation. To be effective, learn and practice marking the list using these indicators.

CLASSROOM SNAPSHOT TOOL INDICATORS

INDICATOR	OPERATIONAL DEFINITION
RESPONSIVE, BRAIN-BASED CLASSROOMS	
CLASSROOM INSTRUCTIONAL DESIGN	
Varieties of visible print and student work	The classroom surrounds the students in teacher-generated and student-generated print and shows examples of student work that demonstrate expected levels of achievement.
Group areas and open space	The room is arranged to accommodate large and small groups, with enough open space for students to move among groups.
Attractive, rich learning environment	The teacher has created intriguing displays and visuals to stimulate and engage students.
Efficient pacing of instructional time	Instruction is paced to promote high expectations and student engagement, with no inappropriate lags in instruction.
TEACHER INSTRUCTIONAL STRATEGIES	
Varieties of materials and resources	Students have more than one resource to use to complete a task.
Varieties of teacher-directed strategies	The teacher offers multiple learning strategies so students have the opportunity to be successful and achieve the target.
Assessment incorporated into the teaching segment	The teacher informally or formally assesses student learning during the lesson.
Clear teacher instructional communication and instructional sequencing	Verbal cues are clear, and the instruction builds on deliberate sequencing and previous student knowledge to ensure understanding.
STUDENT RESPONSIVENESS	
Student routines and management of own learning	Students follow established routines, appear to understand management expectations, and take responsibility for efficient classroom functioning.
Suitable, appropriate student movement	Students move easily and quickly into different instructional groupings when directed.

CLASSROOM SNAPSHOT TOOL INDICATORS continued

INDICATOR	OPERATIONAL DEFINITION
ENGAGING STUDENT TASKS	
CONTENT DESIGN	
Respectful tasks for all students	All students, regardless of ability, are assigned appropriate tasks that respect their capabilities and encourage their engagement.
Focus on student understanding	The teacher's dialogue, questions, and required tasks focus on students' understanding of the content, not simply covering the content.
Inquiry- and/or experience-based	Instruction is focused on students' natural inquisitiveness and overtly connects with students' experiences.
Focus on real-world applications	The instructional focus is on the usefulness of the content or skill in out-of-classroom experiences.
Differentiation of content, process, and/or product	The instruction is differentiated either in terms of what the student should know or be able to do, the kinds of activities asked of the student, or how the student will demonstrate proficiency.
CONTENT DELIVERY	
Purposeful student conversation with the teacher	The teacher's communication with students is focused on natural inquiry, identifying similarities and differences, and/or generating thinking.
Evidence of student engagement in task	Students appear to be cognitively, behaviorally, and emotionally connected to the learning.
Seamless use of materials	The teacher's materials are organized in a way to enhance the efficiency of the instruction.
Varieties of instructional groupings	The teacher uses a variety of instructional arrangements, such as whole-group, individual, paired, and small-group instruction as appropriate.

National Staff Development Council

CLASSROOM SNAPSHOT TOOL INDICATORS continued

INDICATOR	OPERATIONAL DEFINITION
COMMUNITY OF RESPECT AND LEARNING	
CULTURAL RESPONSIVENESS	
Overall culture of fairness and equality	The teacher's instruction, classroom setting, and management support a culture of equality and opportunity for students.
Respectful teacher directions	The teacher's questions and dialogue with students are focused yet supportive and encouraging.
Established and fair student routines	Student routines are equitable, easily understood, and administered evenhandedly.
Teacher capitalization on student interests	The teacher's instruction is flexible, and the teacher uses "teachable moments" to focus on individual student responses and experiences.
Teacher-student connections	The teacher's behavior, questions, and responses underscore a desire to maintain strong teacher-student connections.
CLASSROOM STANDARDS	
Visuals indicating class guidelines or desired social behaviors	Desired social or management behaviors are posted in the classroom.
Room arrangement to support student and teacher community	The room is arranged in a way to support discussion, sharing of ideas, and joint investigation.
Daily learning goals posted for student and teacher view	The teacher posts the day's learning goals and uses them to target and focus instruction.

Get an accurate classroom snapshot

This example explains the thinking required to accurately complete a classroom snapshot:

Marisol Norales, the specialist, observes that at the beginning of the visit, the teacher's pacing of the large-group mathematics lesson keeps students on task and engaged. However, about eight minutes into the visit, the teacher spends a great deal of time answering one student's question, and other students appear to lose interest. Norales notices that six to eight students begin to doodle, read something else, or find another quiet activity. During Norales' visit, the teacher does not quickly find materials to transition to the last math activity, further slowing the pacing. So, although the teacher's pacing was efficient about half of the time, these two teacher actions caused a significant number of students to disengage and jeopardized the lesson's effectiveness. The specialist marks "no" for "efficient pacing of instructional time," one of the indicators under the header "classroom instructional design."

While the classroom snapshot indicators are separate items, they often are related in ways that the specialist will discover during use. In this example, the teacher's lack of materials preparation led Norales to mark "no" on the pacing indicator, but she also then may decide to check "no" on "seamless use of materials" and, if she saw a lack of student engagement throughout the lesson in numbers that seemed significant, for that indicator as well.

Teachers sometimes ask for copies of the completed snapshot, but this tool is most valuable when used for aggregated data about several classrooms. If the specialist and the leadership team have communicated effectively, the teacher will not expect to receive a copy of the checklist. If a teacher feels a compelling need to see the individual snapshot, check with the principal or leadership team before sharing the completed individual tool with that teacher.

Patterns

The sample Classroom Snapshot Tool shows how it looks when completed. Note the completed classroom snapshot and the patterns of tallies.
- If you were the school-based specialist, how would you look at this completed tool?
- Is there a relationship among the indicators? Does it appear that some aspects of the teacher's planning and decision making are related?
- How would you summarize the snapshot of this teacher?

CLASSROOM SNAPSHOT TOOL TALLY

Date and time _10/21/08_   School _Greentree Elementary_   Grade _6_   Subject _Math_

Classroom teacher _Teacher Example_   Classroom activity during observation _large group – inequalities_

RESPONSIVE, BRAIN-BASED CLASSROOMS	YES	NO
CLASSROOM INSTRUCTIONAL DESIGN		
Varieties of visible print and student work	✓	
Group areas and open space	✓	
Attractive, rich learning environment	✓	
Efficient pacing of instructional time		✓
TEACHER INSTRUCTIONAL STRATEGIES		
Varieties of materials and resources	✓	
Varieties of teacher-directed strategies	✓	
Assessment incorporated into the teaching segment	✓	
Clear teacher instructional communication and instructional sequencing	✓	
STUDENT RESPONSIVENESS	✓	
Student routines and management of own learning	✓	
Suitable, appropriate student movement		

ENGAGING STUDENT TASKS	YES	NO
CONTENT DESIGN		
Respectful tasks for all students	✓	
Focus on student understanding	✓	
Inquiry- and/or experience-based	✓	
Focus on real-world applications	✓	
Differentiation of content, process, and/or product	✓	
CONTENT DELIVERY		
Purposeful student conversation with the teacher		✓
Evidence of student engagement in task		✓
Seamless use of materials		✓
Varieties of instructional groupings		✓

COMMUNITY OF RESPECT AND LEARNING	YES	NO
CULTURAL RESPONSIVENESS		
Overall culture of fairness and equality	✓	
Respectful teacher directions	✓	
Established and fair student routines	✓	
Teacher capitalization on student interests	✓	
Teacher-student connections	✓	
CLASSROOM STANDARDS		
Visuals indicating class guidelines or desired social behaviors	✓	
Room arrangement to support student and teacher community	✓	
Daily learning goals posted for student and teacher view	✓	

NOTES: _Delays in instructional pacing – materials were not ready – teacher connection was often focused on "yes"/"no" response._

The exchange

The big picture

In the example shown here of a snapshot data display, the elementary school data are displayed according to how frequently (in aggregate) the indicators were observed — more than 70% of the time, 50% to 70% of the time, or less than 50% of the time. The appropriate cell then was shaded. Use color-coded cells to make the chart easier to read at a glance so that team members can easily see which indicators were present and those absent, which will provoke lively discussions.

▪ PLANNING THE EXCHANGE

The snapshot provides interesting, aggregated, visual data that will result in exchanges about classroom practices among teachers and allow them to explore their collective vision for quality classrooms.

After completing multiple snapshots in a given day at a school, aggregate the data using a simple spreadsheet or table. A simple way to compile the data is to use a blank copy of the snapshot and tally the "yes" and "no" marks for each indicator from the individual classroom sheets, painting a school profile for multiple classrooms on a particular day.

The next step is to decide how to visually display the aggregated results. Experiment with different methods of displaying data for the particular school's team to create a visual that will be clear and easy for recipients to understand.

CLASSROOM SNAPSHOT TOOL DATA

Greentree Elementary School

Indicator	>70%	50%<70%	<50%
RESPONSIVE, BRAIN-BASED CLASSROOMS			
CLASSROOM INSTRUCTIONAL DESIGN			
Varieties of visible print and student work			■
Group areas and open space	■		
Attractive, rich learning environment		■	
Efficient pacing of instructional time			
TEACHER INSTRUCTIONAL STRATEGIES			
Varieties of materials and resources		■	
Varieties of teacher-directed strategies			
Assessment incorporated into the teaching segment			■
Clear teacher instructional communication and instructional sequencing			■
STUDENT RESPONSIVENESS			
Student routines and management of own learning	■		
Suitable, appropriate student movement	■		
ENGAGING STUDENT TASKS			
CONTENT DESIGN			
Respectful tasks for all students	■		
Focus on student understanding			■
Inquiry- and/or experience-based			■
Focus on real-world application			■
Differentiation of content, process, and/or product			■
CONTENT DELIVERY			
Purposeful student conversation with the teacher			■
Evidence of student engagement in task		■	
Seamless use of materials	■		
Varieties of instructional groupings		■	
COMMUNITY OF RESPECT AND LEARNING			
CULTURAL RESPONSIVENESS			
Overall culture of fairness and equality	■		
Respectful teacher directions	■		
Established and fair student routines	■		■
Teacher capitalization on student interests			■
Teacher-student connections			
CLASSROOM STANDARDS		■	
Visuals indicating class guidelines or desired social behaviors	■		
Room arrangement to support student and teacher community			■
Daily learning goals posted for student and teacher view			

■ CONDUCTING THE EXCHANGE

When the display of the aggregated data is complete, talk to the leadership team about the collective school picture and facilitate the resultant inquiry, planning, and professional learning.

In sharing the data with the leadership team, be sure to honor the context of the school and the observations, the relationships of the team members, and the team's desired outcomes. Team members may be drawn, for example, to focus on "absent" indicators, but point out first what the data show is in place to help participants to build on the positive.

Tips for an exchange with the leadership team

The following classroom snapshot exchange conference framework may help in preparing leading questions or statements to begin discussion of the results and to make subsequent decisions. These suggestions for the exchange conference are a synthesis from Costa & Garmston (2002); Downey et al. (2004); and Garmston & Wellman (1999).

CLASSROOM SNAPSHOT TOOL EXCHANGE CONFERENCE
Facilitation prompts for the specialist

INTENT	SUGGESTED REMARKS	ASSUMPTIONS OR GOALS	SUGGESTED PROCESS
Set the stage	"I really enjoyed being in the school on _____ day. It was wonderful to see many classrooms and how teachers were working with the students."	To assume positive intention and establish a fair playing ground.	Have participants sit around tables to invite informal conversation. Foster team members' comfort level by not rushing the debriefing process.
Begin the reflection	"Remember the classroom snapshot and its purpose? Let me tell you about my process and what we agreed we would do."	To set the context for the debriefing and remind the team of the purpose for collecting data.	Share a blank classroom snapshot and review the tool briefly. Ask for questions or thoughts about the day's discussion.
Share	"Let me share with you what I found on the day I was in classrooms."	To share process by focusing on positive results.	Share any indicators that were observed more than 70% of the time. Discuss. Ask participants to indicate if they have made any effort toward affecting these indicators. Speculate whether professional learning over the past years has affected these indicators. Together build a theory of what has worked.
Invite the group to see all the data	"Are you interested in seeing the rest of the data?"	To determine whether members are ready to dig deeper and begin reflecting/planning.	Share the remaining data showing all of the indicators.

Facilitation prompts for the specialist

INTENT	SUGGESTED REMARKS	ASSUMPTIONS OR GOALS	SUGGESTED PROCESS
Reflect on the data	"What do you see in this display of the compiled data? Why do you suppose some indicators are represented and some aren't?"	To stimulate thought about the cause-effect relationship between the teacher's behavior and student engagement.	Ask participants to silently review the data and/or work in pairs to begin to summarize and develop theories to explain the results. After allotting time for pairs to review the data, encourage the entire team to begin a dialogue.
Reflect on the data	"Why do you think that might be so?" "What are you wondering about?"	To invite analysis.	Engage the team in a dialogue about the data and results. Encourage broad participation and deep discussion by asking "why" after individual members speculate on reasons certain indicators were present or absent.
Plan	"So you are saying that if _____, then _____."	To invite team members to propose theories for change.	At this point, leadership team members may suggest how they would like to communicate the data to and begin a dialogue with the entire staff about a vision for instruction. Or team members may wish to use the data to plan future professional learning or job-embedded ways to continue the conversation about classroom quality.
Finalize a plan	"So you believe that the next steps are to _____."	To finalize the plan.	Ask team members to summarize and verify the tentative plan they began developing.

CLASSROOM SNAPSHOT TOOL EXCHANGE CONFERENCE continued
Facilitation prompts for the specialist

INTENT	SUGGESTED REMARKS	ASSUMPTIONS OR GOALS	SUGGESTED PROCESS
Plan and evaluate	"How would you know if these steps are successful? What would you want to see to tell you the actions you have planned are having the effect you want?"	To plan measures to check progress.	At this point in the conversation, team members likely will need to be pressed to talk about ways to measure the progress of their new initiatives. They may want to consider using the Classroom Snapshot Tool again at a later time and/or consider other measures.
Manage and align	"How do these actions today fit with your school improvement plans?"	To align this conversation and subsequent actions with existing plans and check coherence.	Ask the team to align this plan with school improvement plans to make sure any actions are part of the leadership's overall thinking.
Think ahead	"Let's talk again about the changes you would expect to see on the snapshot if our plan is working."	To reflect on the plan and speculate on changes that the snapshot might capture if used again.	Ask team members to reaffirm their thinking.
Reflect	"Tell me, as you reflect on this process today, what has changed for you?"	To reflect on the entire exchange process and determine the level of positive feelings about the tool, the data, and the process.	Invite members to react to the process and to re-examine the snapshot content and the decisions made during the meeting.
Reflect and close	"When should we have our next conversation about this tool, our plans, and the progress we're tracking?"	To promote the sense that the improvement is ongoing and that periodic attention will be important to sustaining the change.	Commit to the changes and a future date to discuss progress.

DEVELOPING THEORIES AND MAKING COMMITMENTS

At the end of the leadership team exchange and planning session, the specialist will want to capture the team's theories and commitments, compile these notes, and share the information with team members. Each school team will use the results differently.

At Greentree Elementary (see sample charts), the leadership team reviewed the data and discussed implications, then suggested sharing the snapshot data with all the teachers in the school. At a lively meeting of the full faculty, teachers began real dialogue — probably in ways previously unfamiliar to them — about their classroom practices. Many teachers began to make changes in their practices based entirely on their examination of the tool and the supportive whole-faculty dialogue.

NOTES FOR THE BUILDING LEADER

The Classroom Snapshot Tool gives the leadership team and school leaders an efficient and reliable examination of the most promising indicators of quality teaching and learning that are occurring in the school. The tool is not intended to supplant regular teacher evaluation protocols, including informal walk-throughs and more formal devices. It represents one day only in the life of the school — a photograph of what was seen on that day during that time. In looking at the data, leaders should focus on questions such as:

- What patterns appear evident?
- What relationships do you see among the indicators?
- In what ways did the day and time influence how the tool was marked?
- Have teachers been working on any of these practices? How? What results are evident?
- How should we share this information with all teachers?
- What are the implications of this information? How should we move forward?
- What professional learning is suggested? How would the faculty learn best and feel the most supported?

The classroom snapshot is useful for a broad view of a school's overall classroom quality and can help the principal and leadership team align the results of the snapshot with school improvement efforts and professional learning. The tool also is diagnostic and may point the way to areas of need that other tools can help address.

AN EXAMPLE IN PRACTICE

The following details how Greentree Elementary designed the whole-faculty meeting and the results from that meeting:

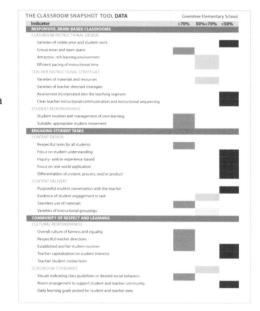

1. The faculty members were all given a copy of the aggregated classroom snapshot results. (See the data display in this chapter.)

2. The school leadership team proposed that four questions guide its analysis for the afternoon:
   - What do you see?
   - Are you already working on any of these practices?
   - What are you wondering about?
   - What do you think our next steps would be to address some of these practices?

3. Faculty members split into working groups, and each group addressed all four questions. Their remarks were captured on large pieces of chart paper.

4. The charts were shared with all in one large gallery walk where faculty members walked around, read each group's comments on the wall, and reflected.

5. The leadership team then facilitated a synthesis of the comments and asked the members to identify areas for work and possible actions to address their own skill and/or information needs.
   - The teachers said many of them were so focused on content delivery that they were often unaware of whether students were engaged.
   - The teachers also hypothesized that the problem was exacerbated by their lack of understanding of what student engagement looked like.

After this meeting, the leadership team compiled teachers' feedback and suggestions and proposed these actions:
- Plan professional learning to help develop an understanding of student engagement.
- Periodically use the Classroom Snapshot Tool to chart any progress in classroom quality over time.
- Encourage teachers to volunteer for the Engagement Visit Tool (see Chapter 4) to begin focusing on their own individual practices to enhance student engagement.

CHAPTER

The ENGAGEMENT VISIT

T O O L

& EXCHANGE

Ben Keller seems like he does a great job in the classroom. Using humor and a high level of energy, Keller sweeps his 3rd graders into their daily tasks through constant chatter, questions, and individual and group work.

Keller's students appear to thoroughly enjoy each day. They joke with him and cheerfully take on responsibilities. After several informal visits to Keller's classroom, though, the school-based specialist notices that Keller broadcasts his content and assignments and rarely stops to see whether students are on task or to check for understanding. Several students appear to be compliant to Keller's instructional requests, but seem only superficially engaged in the work. Keller appears oblivious to these students.

He generally stays in front of the room and doesn't seem to notice how engaged his students are during a typical lesson.

In casual conversation with the specialist, Keller wonders if his teaching strategies are having a real effect on his students. The specialist says she has a tool to help look at Keller's teaching behaviors and the behaviors of targeted students. Keller says he would love to see this kind of data and asks for more information.

Keller obviously enjoys teaching and wants his students to be their best. He also seems to enjoy a trusting relationship with his school-based specialist. The Engagement Visit Tool will let the two explore how Keller can find which of his practices engages students, decide ways to increase student engagement, and track how his student engagement changes over time.

THE ENGAGEMENT VISIT TOOL

Date and time _____ School _____ Grade _____ Subject _____

Classroom teacher _____ Classroom activity during observation _____

STUDENT NAMES					NOTES
ENGAGEMENT VISIT: ENGAGING TEACHER ACTIONS AND BEHAVIORS					
Call on student					
Latency 5+					
Help					
Delve					
Higher-level questions and extensions					
Affirmation					
Specific praise					
Listen					
Accept feelings					
Proximity to student (teacher-initiated)					
Seek student ideas, thoughts, opinions					
Courtesy					
Personal interest or connection to student					
Touch					
Desist					
STUDENT ACTIONS AND BEHAVIORS					
Raise hand					
Ask the teacher a question					
Answer teacher's question, respond					
Follow teacher's direction					
Proximity to teacher (student-initiated)					
Active listening to teacher (look at)					
Check in					
Off task with a peer					
Off task alone					
Disrupting others					

Teacher addresses whole class (tally): _____

Additional information: _____

The Institute for Excellence in Urban Education, a program of the Salesmanship Club Youth and Family Centers, contributed to the development of this tool.

INSIGHTS

As Phillip Schlechty states, "One of the first steps in moving toward continuously improving the quality of the work provided to students is to center attention on the patterns of engagement in a classroom or set of classrooms" (2002, p. 8). Schlechty suggests that an engagement profile of the classroom helps educators focus on the dynamic relationship between teacher and learner.

Researchers from the Institute for Excellence in Urban Education and the J. Erik Jonsson Community School (both programs of the Dallas, Texas, nonprofit Salesmanship Club Youth and Family Centers) developed a tool to gauge students' engagement in the classroom. Called the Engagement Visit Tool, the tool is divided into two parts:

- 15 positive teacher behaviors and actions, drawn from the Teacher Expectations and Student Achievement (TESA) research, which have a positive impact on student engagement (Cantor, Kester, & Miller, 2000; Gottfredson, Marciniak, Birdseye, & Gottfredson, 1995); and
- 10 student actions and behaviors that, collectively, demonstrate how selected students respond to specific teacher behaviors.

The Engagement Visit Tool shows specific teacher and student behaviors.

A separate student component adds to the Engagement Visit Tool and Exchange between the teacher and specialist. The three or four students targeted during the observation consider their own levels of engagement using the student self-rating of engagement.

SELECTING PARTICIPANTS

Any teacher who wants to learn more about which practices engage students is a good candidate for this tool. The teacher or school-based specialist may identify up to four students to observe, focusing, for example, only on low-achieving students or students with behavior problems. Other reasons to select students are if, for example, the teacher or specialist suspects there are differences in students' engagement in this class based on gender or race.

If there is no compelling reason to select certain students, randomly select three or four, perhaps drawing names before entering the classroom. Focusing on randomly selected students ensures that those students who are acting out or behaving outside the norm are not the only ones observed.

Because the Engagement Visit Tool is used to obtain a routine sampling of teacher-student actions and behaviors under normal circumstances, use the tool several times to get an adequate profile of everyday teacher behaviors and student reactions.

BUILDING TRUST

Before visiting the classroom, share all of the materials and procedures of the Engagement Visit Tool so the teacher is aware of what will be observed and recorded. Stress that all the data will be provided to the teacher before the exchange conversation, and that the conversation will be about patterns of teacher actions, student behaviors, and subsequent evidence of student engagement.

Some teachers, even if they have volunteered for the Engagement Visit Tool, may be reluctant to begin the process. They may think the specialist will share the results with the building principal (for evaluation purposes) or will judge the teacher's behaviors. Be clear that the tool will not be used for evaluation and that the results will be a catalyst for conversation and, hopefully, a device for professional growth and enhanced practice.

Get to know the students in the participating teacher's classroom before beginning the observations. One way to do this is to visit the classroom informally, without paper or pencil, to help students feel comfortable. During the classroom observation, the teacher and students must be able to work without being distracted by the observer's presence. Also share the student self-rating of engagement form with the class and discuss what "engaged" means. This small amount of preparation will go a long way in helping students accurately complete the student self-rating if they are asked.

■ DECIDING TO USE THE TOOL

Use the Engagement Visit Tool:

- To measure the relationship between teacher behaviors and student engagement;
- If the teacher is interested in learning how engaged students are in their lessons;
- When the teacher's students do not seem engaged in the work;
- When the school-based specialist and teacher are concerned about specific students and whether their lack of performance is linked to a low level of engagement in classroom instruction; and/or
- If the school leadership team is curious about evidence of student engagement in the majority of the school's classes and whether overall school improvement plans are accelerating and sustaining student engagement.

The Engagement Visit Tool is not to be used as another measure for teacher evaluation. It is intended to gather data about the relationship of teacher behaviors to student behaviors, build a strong relationship between a specialist and teacher exchanging information about teaching practices, and to focus the teacher on changes in his or her behavior that might spark deeper and more sustained student engagement in classroom tasks.

Checklist of materials for the Engagement Visit Tool

- ☐ One student self-rating of engagement form for each observed student
- ☐ One Engagement Visit Tool for each observation session
- ☐ Clipboard or hard writing surface
- ☐ Extra pencils or pens
- ☐ Class seating chart or class photo
- ☐ Timing device or watch

Student self-assessment

A separate student component adds to the Engagement Visit Tool and Exchange.

One form is for elementary school students, and a different form may be used for middle and high school students. The teacher and specialist use the data from these forms and the Engagement Visit Tool results during the exchange conference.

ELEMENTARY SCHOOL STUDENT **SELF-RATING OF ENGAGEMENT**

Name:_____ Date:_____

Teacher:_____

WHAT JUST HAPPENED?

Check ✓ only one.

	I was really engaged in my class work. The lesson is important to me. I care about what my teacher asks me to do.
	I paid attention in class and did my work. I want to get good grades. The lesson did not seem important to me. I did my work because I was asked to do it.
	I did some of my work. I did some of my work and stayed out of trouble.
	I was bored. I did not do my work. I did not cause trouble.
	I did not do my work. I got in trouble in class because I did not do my work. I don't plan to change what I am doing.

MIDDLE OR HIGH SCHOOL SCHOOL STUDENT **SELF-RATING OF ENGAGEMENT**

Name:_____ Date:_____

Teacher:_____

Looking back over the lesson, which of the following statements most closely reflects the way you approached the work your teacher assigned you?

Check ✓only one.

	I have been really interested in the work and in my class. I generally do what I am asked to do because I see how the class work relates to things I care about.
	I always pay attention in class and do the work I am assigned because I want to get good grades, but I really don't see much use in what I am asked to do, and I might not do it if I didn't feel I had to.
	I do what I need to do to get by, but I really only put out as much effort as I have to in order to stay out of trouble.
	I am bored and haven't done much work for my class, but I haven't caused any trouble for my teacher.
	I have been in some trouble because I haven't done what the teacher wants me to do, but that's just the way it goes. I don't plan to change what I'm doing.

■ USING THE TOOL

Fifteen minutes to 20 minutes of continuous observation will yield enough data about teacher and student behaviors for one observation period. Schedule several observations over time to get reliable information about teacher-student behaviors and to provide ongoing information during exchange conversations with the teacher to spark the teacher's enthusiasm and efforts to engage students.

Stay mobile during the observation to be able to see each targeted student from at least the side, but preferably from the front. Moving around during the observation helps to capture teacher actions, student behaviors, and individual conversations between the teacher and the targeted students.

Schedule the first engagement visit observation by giving the teacher an exact day and time to allow the teacher to anticipate the first visit. Whether subsequent observations are scheduled or unscheduled, teachers should not make special accommodations or alter their routines during the observations since the idea is to capture typical actions.

In marking either the teacher actions or student behaviors, one action or behavior may trigger a tally mark for an additional, related behavior. For instance, "listen" and "accept feelings" may occur simultaneously. If so, put a tally mark next to both indicators for the related behaviors.

When the observation time is over, give a rating sheet immediately to each targeted student and collect the rating sheets before students leave the classroom. The intent of the student self-ratings is to derive each student's level of engagement and/or interest in the classroom activity during the observed time. Ask the student to complete the heading and to circle the rating that best describes his or her level of engagement in "what just happened when I (the observer) was in the classroom with you."

Tool tips

List targeted student names across the top of the Engagement Visit Tool. As the teacher exhibits one of the listed behaviors, place a check in the box below the targeted student's name in the appropriate row. Tally only those teacher behaviors that are directed toward the targeted students. Teacher behaviors directed toward other students in the class or the class as a whole may be tallied at the bottom of the form.

Record students' actions and behaviors during the same observation. As the targeted student demonstrates one of the listed actions and behaviors, check the box under his or her name next to the observed behavior.

The final three categories of student behaviors are the student's attention to the task — either "on task" or "off task." Note these behaviors whether or not the teacher is aware that the student is off task or disrupting another.

Practice the indicators

Practice recording both teacher and student behaviors in pilot settings before completing an observation with the participating teacher. Practice is crucial to completing the form, because teachers' behaviors often occur in a rapid sequence, making them difficult to document. Prepare by becoming completely familiar with the definitions of teacher and student behaviors listed in the tool. Operational definitions of the observable teacher actions and behaviors are listed here.

ENGAGEMENT VISIT TOOL INDICATORS
TEACHER ACTIONS AND BEHAVIORS

INDICATOR	OPERATIONAL DEFINITION
Call on student	The teacher provides an individual response opportunity to the student by calling on, nodding toward, or signaling to the student. The teacher may acknowledge the student by name to the class as well.
Latency 5+	The teacher poses a question and waits before speaking for five or more seconds (5+) for the individual student to respond. The teacher allows the student time to think the question over before the teacher terminates the response opportunity or assists the student.
Help	The teacher gives the student individual assistance in response to a student's request for help, or the aid can be teacher-initiated. The "help" can be anything, including instructional help or materials.
Delve	The teacher rephrases or provides any additional information verbally or nonverbally to assist the student in responding to a question or prompt. The need often occurs when students provide partial answers, require redirection, or want clarification.
Higher-level questions and extensions	The teacher asks the student a question that requires him or her to do something more than merely remember the answer. These questions require the student to apply, synthesize, or evaluate previous knowledge to determine a correct response or the next action.
Affirmation	The teacher acknowledges the work, response, or action of an individual student to that student or to the entire class. Affirmation is a way of honoring the student's thinking and/or actions.
Specific praise	The teacher praises the student's thinking, work, or behavior — with specific reasons why he or she is praising it. The praise can be either directly to that student or about the student to other members of the class.
Listen	The teacher maintains eye contact with the individual student or indicates to the student that the particular response was heard and understood.

INDICATOR	OPERATIONAL DEFINITION
Accept feelings	The teacher is seen to recognize and accept a student's feelings in a non-evaluative, supportive manner.
Proximity to student (teacher-initiated)	The teacher comes within one arm's reach of a targeted student, whether or not the student is aware of the teacher's presence.
Seek student ideas, thoughts, opinions	The teacher probes and questions to spark inquiry or to attach personal interest to the activity or task.
Courtesy	The teacher uses expressions of courtesy in interactions with the individual student. The teacher uses words such as *please, thank you, I appreciate your attention to the project*, etc.
Personal interest or connection to student	The teacher asks questions or makes statements referring to the student's personal interests, experiences, family, or home.
Touch	The teacher touches the student in an intentional and supportive manner. The teacher's touch can be a demonstration of warm regard or used to redirect a student's behavior.
Desist	The teacher asks the student to desist from a behavior in a calm, courteous manner that does not demean the student. The "desist" action can be a touch (see above) or a facial expression or gesture that is directed to the individual student. The desist action clearly directs the student to stop his or her current behavior.

ENGAGEMENT VISIT TOOL INDICATORS
STUDENT ACTIONS AND BEHAVIORS

INDICATOR	OPERATIONAL DEFINITION
Raise hand	The student raises his or her hand in response to the teacher's question or to get the teacher's attention or ask for assistance.
Ask the teacher a question	The student asks the teacher a question about the lesson or activity. This act can co-occur with the student's proximity to the teacher, the teacher's proximity to the student, or the question might be asked across the room. This student action is counted as *ask a question* even if the teacher does not acknowledge it. The question should be related to the task, not a general question, such as, "Can I go to the restroom?"
Answer teacher's question, respond	The student answers a question posed by the teacher to the individual student, to the student group, or to the entire class. Note: If the teacher asks a question, and the student raises his hand, the action counts as *raise hand* and is counted for *answer the teacher's question* if that student did respond with an answer.
Follow teacher's direction	The student follows a specific directive addressed to either the particular student or to the entire class.
Proximity to teacher (student-initiated)	The student approaches the teacher within one arm's length. If the teacher approaches the student, it is counted as *proximity to student*.
Active listening to teacher (look at)	The student acknowledges the teacher when the teacher speaks. This acknowledgement includes such behaviors as eye contact, nod, smile, etc. — in an overt way to demonstrate to the teacher that the student is attending to what the teacher is saying.

INDICATOR	OPERATIONAL DEFINITION
Check in	The student glances toward the teacher or searches out the teacher's activity when the teacher is not engaged with the student, his group, or the entire class. This *checking in* can indicate simple curiosity about the teacher's whereabouts. Checking in usually happens without the teacher's awareness.
Off task with a peer	The student and one or more others are engaged in off-task activity. It may be observed as students playing around together or a collaborative inattention to the task.
Off task alone	The student is unfocused and is seen daydreaming but does not disrupt other students. Off-task, alone behavior can include very intent behavior on a task that is not related to the classroom expectation at the time.
Disrupting others	The student is off task, fooling around, and disrupting his neighbor's attention to the task. This behavior is different from off task with a peer in that in disrupting, the peer is not joining in with the behavior; in fact, the student is being disrupted from remaining on task by the off-task student.

Reflect on the data

Here is an example of a completed Engagement Visit Tool. Note the tally marks and notes.

What patterns, if any, do you notice? How would you prepare for this exchange conference?

ENGAGEMENT VISIT TOOL TALLY

Date and time _9/26/07 9:44-9:59_ School _____ Grade _2nd_ Subject _writing + LA_

Classroom teacher _____ Classroom activity during observation _____

Student names	Martin	Aron	Carla	Natalie	Notes
ENGAGEMENT VISIT: ENGAGING TEACHER ACTIONS AND BEHAVIORS					
Call on student		//	/		
Latency 5+					
Help	//	~~THL~~	//		
Delve		/			
Higher-level questions and extensions					
Affirmation		//			
Specific praise		//			
Listen	/	////			
Accept feelings					
Proximity to student (teacher-initiated)		/			
Seek student ideas, thoughts, opinions	_would you like to?_	//			
Courtesy		//			
Personal interest or connection to student					
Touch					
Desist			//		
STUDENT ACTIONS AND BEHAVIORS					
Raise hand					
Ask the teacher a question	//	///	//		
Answer teacher's question, respond	/	//			
Follow teacher's direction	//	/	/		
Proximity to teacher (student-initiated)	//	/			
Active listening to teacher (look at)		/			
Check in	//	//	/		_copying off neighbor's work?_
Off task with a peer	///	//		// ↙	
Off task alone	/	/		~~THL~~	
Disrupting others	_at desk distracted_	_wk w/ Tchr for 5 mins then at desk_	_math game w/ partner_	_at desk then gets a book on the floor_	

Teacher addresses whole class (tally): _____

Additional information: _____

The Institute for Excellence in Urban Education, a program of the Salesmanship Club Youth and Family Centers, contributed to the development of this tool.

The exchange

toward students?

- Were any of the targeted students highly engaged? Why or why not?
- Were students of all races equally engaged?
- Were students of both genders equally engaged?
- Were students of all abilities equally and consistently engaged?
- If any of the targeted students went off task, what was happening in the classroom at that moment?
- How did the targeted students assess their own levels of engagement? Were their self-ratings similar to the specialist's ratings of them?
- How might you surface ideas to consider in a way that both honors the teacher and provides fodder during the exchange conference?

▨ PLANNING THE EXCHANGE

The completed Engagement Visit Tool will reveal an interesting picture of the relationship between teacher and student behaviors. However, the most powerful by-product is the exchange conference, where teacher and specialist talk about the classroom visit. Have the exchange conference as quickly as possible after visiting the classroom. The teacher will naturally be curious about the observation and will want to discover any insights that might lead to classroom improvement. At the exchange conference, provide copies of the completed Engagement Visit Tool and all four student self-rating sheets for the teacher to keep.

In preparing for the exchange conference, reflect on these points and questions:

- Look at the sum of all of the tallies for the classroom visit. What do the numbers mean? What questions do you have or what do you wonder about the tallies and your observations in the classroom?
- Did the teacher behave differently toward the observed students? If so, how?
- Did the teacher display general patterns of behavior that generate questions for the specialist?
- Did any student grouping affect the teacher's behavior

Tips for the exchange conference

In general, the sequential conversation starters in the engagement visit exchange conference framework may be used to proceed from the beginning of the exchange conference to its conclusion. These suggestions for the exchange conference are a synthesis from Costa & Garmston (2002); Downey et al. (2004); and Garmston & Wellman (1999).

▨ CONDUCTING THE EXCHANGE

The goal of the exchange conference is to facilitate and support the teacher's thinking about ways to better engage students in learning. To accomplish this goal, plan carefully to build a trusting relationship with the teacher and to share data to encourage teachers to change their actions so students are more consistently and deeply engaged every day in the classroom.

Joellen Killion and Cindy Harrison, in *Taking the*

ENGAGEMENT VISIT TOOL EXCHANGE CONFERENCE
Facilitation prompts for the specialist

INTENT	SUGGESTED REMARKS	ASSUMPTIONS OR GOALS
Set the stage	"I really enjoyed being in your class today. It was great to see you work with your kids."	Assume positive presupposition and establish a fair playing ground. Establish a positive, collegial tone.
Begin the reflection	"What do you think of your lesson? How do you think it went?"	Pose an open-ended question that allows the teacher to take the lead in interpreting the lesson.
Reflect	"Talk with me about what was going on when I was there."	Provide the teacher an opportunity to talk about his or her emotional reactions, bring up any factors that he/she noticed, etc.
Reflect	"Did you get the results you wanted?"	Ask the teacher to analyze the results of the lesson from his/her perspective *and* focus on the students.
Reflect on the data	"Are you interested in seeing the student engagement data?" (Give out the engagement visit form.)	Ask the teacher if he/she is ready to see the data, and hand the data to the teacher to begin to analyze.
Reflect on the data	"What do you see or notice here? What are your first reactions?"	Invite the teacher to begin to capture the big ideas of the data and what they might represent.
Reflect on the data	"What patterns do you notice? Are there relationships among any of the indicators?"	Prime the teacher to see the relationship of the indicators or to look at overall results.
Reflect on the data	"What you are seeing and what you are telling me is _____."	Paraphrase to stimulate ideas about the cause-effect relationship between the teacher's behaviors and student engagement.
Reflect on the data	"Why do you think that might be so?"	Invite analysis.
Plan	"You are saying that if you _____, then _____."	Invite the teacher to plan and act on his or her own theory for improvement.
Plan	"In what ways would this enhance the kind of engagement you are seeking?"	Connect the proposed teacher actions to theorized student behaviors.
Plan	"The next time I'm here, you would like for me to _____ while you are _____."	Finalize the plan and confirm the focus for the next engagement observation.
Reflecting	"Tell me, as you reflect on this process today, what does it do for you?"	Reflect on the exchange process and determine the extent of positive feelings for the next conversation.

Lead: New Roles for Teachers and School-Based Coaches (NSDC, 2006), advise that school-based specialists often take on integrated roles such as resource provider, data coach, and classroom supporter. During the exchange conference, the teacher may be at a loss about how to begin to change his or her behaviors. During the exchange conference, then, the school-based specialist may be asked to provide resources or consult with the teacher in one or more of Killion's and Harrison's roles so the teacher might later be able to apply his or her knowledge and assume more responsibility for improved student engagement.

DEVELOPING THEORIES AND MAKING COMMITMENTS

Helping the teacher articulate a theory for action is the most critical part of a productive exchange conference. As the teacher reflects on the data, listen carefully to questions the teacher poses, such as, "I wonder what would happen if …" or "I suppose that if I …" These often-overlooked comments are the kernels of a theory of what might happen if the teacher adjusts his or her behavior, attempts more engaging behaviors, or shifts his or her classroom instructional practices to deliberately deepen student engagement. When the teacher seems to be homing in on a theory of instructional improvement through adjusted practices and behaviors, focus the teacher's comments and wonderings by paraphrasing, clarifying, and using confirming statements such as:

- "So you are saying that if you _____, then _____?"

and/or

- "So you are thinking that if you focused on _____, your students would be more engaged?"

and/or

- "Why do you think these changes in your actions would trigger more engaged student behaviors?"

Document the general conversation and any questions raised during the exchange conference. Use these compiled notes to track and monitor any decisions made during the conversation and to guide planning for the next observation with the participating teacher.

Toward the end of the exchange conference, the teacher will seem to have his or her own theory about what to change to more effectively engage students. Confirm the teacher's theory and ensure that the teacher is committed to taking action by inviting the teacher to finalize a plan. Use a statement such as, "So you are going to begin to _____," or "So the next time I'm here, you would like for me to look for _____." If the teacher agrees with the proposed action and is comfortable with his or her theory of improvement, restate what will happen to ensure the teacher appears committed to the theory and the resulting actions.

As with any of the tools, conclude the exchange conference by asking the participating teacher to reflect on the engagement process and the exchange conference. Note any reflections and decisions, and remind the participating teacher when the next classroom visit will take place to look at engagement again.

Note: At any point in the relationship with the participating teacher, reflect on the use of the tool and whether it is the most effective one to be using. If, for instance, the teacher appears to create problematic lesson designs or has overarching disciplinary and or management issues, consider using the Instructional Design Tool (Chapter 5) or the Instructional Management Tool (Chapter 7).

The Engagement Visit Tool is based on the assumptions that the participating teacher is interested in achieving more profound and sustained engagement with his or her class and has the knowledge and resources to determine how his or her behaviors might need to change to engage the students more deeply.

NOTES FOR THE BUILDING LEADER

Results from the Engagement Visit Tool should never be used for formal teacher evaluations. Aside from supporting individual teacher reflection and accomplishment, use the data from the Engagement Visit Tool to look at an aggregate of teacher behaviors and patterns of student behaviors that indicate how engaged students are in the classrooms of the school. The aggregated engagement visit data will be particularly provocative and useful for the school leadership team as it analyzes schoolwide data.

Consider these tips for using aggregated Engagement Visit Tool data:

- Ask the school-based specialist to total all of the tallies for the targeted students. What behavior patterns are evident?

- Ask the school-based specialist to sum all of the participating teachers' tallies across each teacher action and behavior. Do teachers exhibit certain behaviors more regularly? Are some behaviors absent? Should staff explore the pedagogy behind these teacher behaviors during professional learning time for the school?

- If the school-based specialist has been looking at engagement differences between genders or among diverse groups of students, ask for a total of the tallies by group. What do the data show about relative engagement for these groups of students? Why?

Use the analysis of the aggregated data to focus the leadership team's planning and possible professional learning decisions. For instance, if evidence shows that teachers are not frequently or consistently using "higher-level questions and extensions," teachers may benefit from ongoing learning and support on how to implement this desired behavior. After teachers take part in some professional learning around a topic or area, the school-based specialist can track any changes or improvements in behavior and engagement during subsequent engagement visit observations.

5

CHAPTER

The INSTRUCTIONAL DESIGN

T O O L

& EXCHANGE

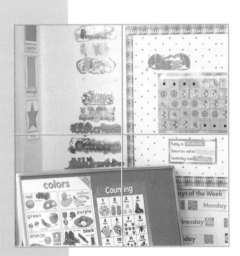

Jennifer Jackson is a first-year teacher at Langley High School. As with many new teachers, Jackson has spent the first part of the school year immersed in learning school procedures, finding materials, attempting discipline management techniques, and teaching content. A little overwhelmed, Jackson bravely begins each day with lesson plans in hand. She feels that many of her lessons go "as expected," but at the same time, she is disappointed in her students' responses. They don't always follow her instructions or complete the assigned tasks. Jackson has tried hands-on and group activities to encourage student interest, conversation, and desire to learn. The students' responses to even these efforts vary. Jackson is frustrated and can't seem to find a way to simultaneously motivate, support, and manage her students. The school-based instructional specialist, as part of his responsibilities, stops by Jackson's classroom one morning to ask how it's going. Jackson gives him an earful, then asks for his help in thinking through her instructional planning.

THE INSTRUCTIONAL DESIGN TOOL

Date and time _____ School _____ Grade _____ Subject _____

Classroom teacher _____ Classroom activity during observation _____

A responsive and respectful learning environment	Yes	No	Notes
CLASSROOM DESIGN			
Attractive, print-rich setting			
Visible evidence of student cultures and a student "voice"			
Varieties of visuals and student work			
Physical grouping areas and open space for flexibility and communication among students			
Written and posted class guidelines or desired social behaviors			
Daily learning goals posted for class understanding			
Easily accessible, multisensory materials and supplies for all students			
LEARNING DESIGN			
Plans include instructional novelty or emotion			
Respectful and important tasks for all students			
Flexible, intentional clusters or groupings for instruction			
Evidence of modification of content, process, and/or product			
Alignment of activities to real-world or student interests			
Evidence of student learning routines and management in the activities			
Suitable, appropriate, student movement during activities			

Additional information:

_____

_____

_____

National Staff Development Council

■ INSIGHTS

Jackson's situation demonstrates a basic instructional need: to create a classroom where students are motivated to learn and where students manage their behavior appropriately. As Robert Marzano (2003b) states, "The link between student motivation and achievement is straightforward. If students are motivated to learn the content in a given subject, their achievement in that subject will most likely be good" (p. 144).

The best motivational and engaging lessons do not exist in a vacuum. Students learn in the context of their instructional space, and lessons can succeed or fail depending on the teacher's attention to the environment in which students are expected to function. Jackson is beginning to recognize the connection between carefully crafted lessons focused on motivation and achievement and a secure, well-designed classroom. The key for Jackson is to carefully craft academically stimulating lessons and to attend simultaneously to the classroom design to support this kind of engaged learning.

New teachers are not the only ones who face this design challenge. Many experienced teachers design lessons without paying attention to the context: the learning space. They prepare quality learning experiences but fail to notice how the classroom's physical arrangement can enhance or detract — even derail — the intended learning.

Jackson is facing the two-pronged challenge of designing both classroom and learning. She needs support to create lessons that are motivational, engaging, and use the classroom space to its highest potential. The challenge is to work with Jackson and teachers with similar needs to look at the interrelationship of lessons and space. The Instructional Design Tool can help analyze where a teacher most needs support to meet the challenge. Any teacher willing to examine his or her lessons and classroom design will reap rewards from the tool's data and subsequent conversations with the school-based specialist.

The Instructional Design Tool can be completed in 15 minutes to 20 minutes of classroom observation. The tool focuses on the teacher's thinking in two areas:

- **Classroom design:** In what ways has the teacher designed the classroom environment to promote high levels of learning and well-managed students?
- **Learning design:** How does the teacher design lessons that make the best use of the classroom space and promote conditions that lead to higher levels of motivation and achievement?

The Instructional Design Tool focuses on the products of the teacher's design "thinking" and what is either observed in the classroom or observed through teacher actions. The majority of the tool's design indicators focus on whether the teacher's actions and classroom design motivate and engage students by providing:

- An attractive, print-rich setting;
- Visible evidence of student work;
- Daily learning goals posted for class understanding;
- Easily accessible, multisensory materials and supplies for all students;
- Plans that include novelty or emotion;
- Respectful and important tasks for all students;
- Flexible, intentional clusters or groupings for instruction;
- Evidence of modified content, process, and/or product; and
- Activities aligned to real-world or student interests.

A few of the 14 indicators examine whether teachers' actions or intentions lead to desired student interactions and management:

- Physical grouping areas and open space for flexibility and communication among students;
- Visible evidence of student cultures and "voice";
- Written and posted class guidelines or desired social behaviors;
- Suitable, appropriate student movement during activities; and
- Evidence of student learning routines and management in the activities.

The tool is a simple checklist with "yes" and "no" columns and a space for notes to document specific ways the teacher created a learning experience for students.

■ DECIDING TO USE THE TOOL

The Instructional Design Tool is meant to help teachers reflect on two correlated concepts — classroom design and learning design. Consider using the Instructional Design Tool when the specialist or teacher:

- Would like to examine whether the way student learning experiences are created is affecting instruction;
- Is interested in whether design or management issues are affecting how instruction is delivered;
- Identifies inconsistent student responses to the teacher's learning plans;
  Or if the teacher:
- Wants to have a dialogue about lesson planning;
- Asks for help in examining and changing the design of the classroom space to promote higher and more sustained student learning.

If the teacher or specialist has questions about the appropriateness of the Instructional Design Tool, he or she should discuss the *nature* of the central issue to be addressed. This conversation often will shed light on which tool to use and the kind of support most likely to be helpful. For example:

- If students aren't achieving and are routinely off task or disruptive, the Instructional Design Tool may not be the most effective. Use the Instructional Management Tool (see Chapter 7) to pinpoint a source of the disruptive behavior.
- If the teacher's or specialist's greatest concern is whether students are engaged, use the Engagement Visit Tool (see Chapter 4) to first look at the relationship between the teacher's actions and student behaviors.

Use the Instructional Design Tool only with teachers who want to study their lesson and classroom design *and* who want to have a dialogue with a colleague about ways to improve. The results should *not* be used for evaluation, but for the teacher to reflect and plan for improved student learning. Be sure teachers and administrators understand that individual teachers' results will be kept confidential and will not be reported to those in evaluative positions.

Checklist of materials for the Instructional Design Tool

- ☐ One Instructional Design Tool for each teacher
- ☐ Clipboard or hard writing surface
- ☐ Extra pencils or pens
- ☐ Timing device or watch
- ☐ Class photos or roster (optional)

Practice the indicators

To complete the tool accurately and effectively, learn the operational definitions for the indicators in advance. Practice completing the tool with another specialist in a volunteer's classroom to compare indicator markings and test reliability.

INSTRUCTIONAL DESIGN TOOL INDICATORS

INDICATOR	OPERATIONAL DEFINITION
CLASSROOM DESIGN	
Attractive, print-rich setting	Numerous classroom displays of instructional print are designed to spark interest and learning.
Visible evidence of student cultures and a student "voice"	The teacher displays work that represents the students, their interests, opinions, and cultures. Other artifacts may showcase students, their families, etc.
Varieties of visuals and student work	A variety of student work demonstrating high standards and examples of high achievement is on display.
Physical grouping areas and open space for flexibility and communication among students	The teacher has arranged the room into multiple areas for learning, including open space for movement and spaces that can be used for small groups and/or individual learning stations.
Written and posted class guidelines or desired social behaviors	Standards for behavior are clearly written in enough detail for students to understand.
Daily learning goals posted for class understanding	The teacher has posted learning objectives (such as "what we are going to accomplish today") for students to see.
Easily accessible, multisensory materials and supplies for all students	The teacher has prepared a variety of multisensory materials and supplies that are readily accessible to the students.
LEARNING DESIGN	
Plans include instructional novelty or emotion	The teacher uses humor, inquiry, surprise, or novelty in the lesson.
Respectful and important tasks for all students	The teacher differentiates instruction and makes all tasks required of students meaningful.
Flexible, intentional clusters or groupings for instruction	The teacher changes instructional groupings at least once to permit partner work, group work, small-group work, etc.
Evidence of modification of content, process, and/or product	The teacher modifies instruction either in the learning task itself, how the task is to be accomplished, or the final product.
Alignment of activities to real-world or student interests	The teacher's design focuses on the usefulness of the content and/or skill in out-of-classroom living.
Evidence of student learning routines and management in the activities	Students accomplish their work with efficiency and demonstrate that they have practiced the expected routines.
Suitable, appropriate, student movement during activities	During the lesson, students move when appropriate and pertinent to their needs or the teacher's request.

SELECTING PARTICIPANTS

The Instructional Design Tool offers specialists a glimpse into a teacher's thinking about lesson and classroom design and uses observation data to spark that conversation. Any teacher who is responsible for creating a physical learning space and for instruction is a candidate for using this tool. Sometimes other tools may reveal data that indicate the specialist should use the Instructional Design Tool. In these cases, make a list of all teachers who might benefit from the Instructional Design Tool. Be cautious in asking teachers to be a part of the tool and exchange conferences, because these "volunteered" teachers may be less positive about the observation and the subsequent conversations. The Instructional Design Tool works best when teachers volunteer because they have committed to thinking and understanding more about classroom and learning design.

BUILDING TRUST

Even teachers who have agreed to take part may be concerned about the tool and how it might reflect on their perceived abilities. The tool's formative data are meant to start a conversation that can lead the teacher to decide on changes, adjustments, and more focused thinking about classroom and lesson design. Still, some teachers will see the indicators and discussion as pointing out deficits. Reinforce that the tool simply provides another perspective and information for the classroom teacher and specialist to use to start a conversation about classroom and learning design.

Use these focusing questions to guide trust building before using the Instructional Design Tool.

- Are the selected teachers eager to be observed and to have this discussion?

Reflect on the data

Look at the example of a completed Instructional Design Tool and determine how you would prepare for this conference.

Read the notes, comments, and questions. If you were the school-based specialist working with this teacher, what would you wonder? Do you see a relationship among any of the indicators? How does the completed tool paint a visual of what was probably happening in the classroom?

Since the tool's purpose is to spark a dialogue about how the teacher can design the classroom to best support intended learning, how would you begin the exchange conference?

What would you hope the teacher did with this information? What would be your role in facilitating his thinking?

- Have the teachers seen a blank copy of the tool?
- Have the teachers seen a completed sample tool?
- Do school leaders know they won't see individual teacher results?
- In what ways will members of the school leadership team be informed about the use of the tool and possible aggregated data?
- Do teachers know how the classroom visits will be scheduled?

INSTRUCTIONAL DESIGN TOOL TALLY

Date and time _2/11/08_ School _Abbott Middle School_ Grade _7_ Subject _Language Arts_

Classroom teacher _A. Butler_ Classroom activity during observation _whole-group instruction_

A responsive and respectful learning environment	Yes	No	Notes
CLASSROOM DESIGN			
Attractive, print-rich setting	✓		
Visible evidence of student cultures and a student "voice"		✓	_Little student work is posted_
Varieties of visuals and student work		✓	
Physical grouping areas and open space for flexibility and communication among students	✓		
Written and posted class guidelines or desired social behaviors		✓	
Daily learning goals posted for class understanding		✓	_Space on the board but not completed for the day_
Easily accessible, multisensory materials and supplies for all students	✓		
LEARNING DESIGN			
Plans include instructional novelty or emotion		✓	
Respectful and important tasks for all students	✓		
Flexible, intentional clusters or groupings for instruction		✓	
Evidence of modification of content, process, and/or product		✓	
Alignment of activities to real-world or student interests	✓		_"How many of you like to go to Six Flags? How does this relate to Six Flags?"_
Evidence of student learning routines and management in the activities	✓		
Suitable, appropriate, student movement during activities	✓		_Little movement during whole group_

Additional information: _Teacher used humor to engage students -- used journals, reading materials, etc. but all in whole group., Teacher asked ̶H̶H̶̶l̶l̶ questions related to "why do you think?" or personal interest. At 1:40, ̶H̶H̶̶l̶ students off task (alone)._

▮ USING THE TOOL

After entering the classroom, make contact with the teacher either visually or verbally if appropriate. Briefly sit in one spot to get a sense of what is happening and to make preliminary observations about the classroom design. Depending on the lesson, move around the room to note not only the teacher's learning intent but also the quantity and quality of student work. Completing this tool is a matter of documenting the classroom environment and also closely focusing on the teacher's lesson. Gathering all the information requires being in several parts of the classroom to get a sense of the teacher's intentions and to see evidence of the indicators in the room itself and in students' tasks. For instance, in the classroom design cluster, simply scan the classroom to see if there are "daily learning goals posted for class understanding." Look at students' actual work to see if there are "respectful and important tasks for all students," one of the indicators in the learning design cluster.

If the teacher has not transitioned students into different groupings or activities within the 15 minutes to 20 minutes of the observation, consider spending a few more minutes to see whether the teacher will use a different mode in the lesson. If he or she does not, note the lack of transition to another mode, activity, grouping, or strategy. Providing this kind of information to the teacher will spark conversation during the exchange conference.

The exchange

PLANNING THE EXCHANGE

The Instructional Design Tool is meant to help the teacher learn the relationship between learning design and classroom design. The tool's results generally reveal a pattern or patterns, and these data can lead to productive conversations with the teacher.

After completing the classroom visit, carefully consider all marks and notes on the tool, and begin to plan the conversation with the teacher. Use these questions to help frame the conversation:

- What do the indicators mean, and what relationships are evident between classroom design and learning design indicators?
- In what ways is the classroom design affecting the learning design, or vice versa?
- What else was apparent during the classroom visit? What do the specialist's notes reveal?
- How would the teacher describe the lesson and the results?
- In what ways was the teacher using the classroom space in his or her instruction? In what ways was the space not being used effectively?
- Is this the right tool to be using? Why or why not?

Plan the exchange conference by studying the results of the observation and deciding which big ideas to focus on, then map a broad framework for the dialogue. Conduct the exchange conference as quickly after the visit as possible, and make a copy of the completed Instructional Design Tool for the teacher to keep after the conference.

Tips for the exchange conference

To frame the conversation so teachers own the data and subsequent changes to their design or behavior, carefully frame questions to provoke thinking and demonstrate respect for the teacher as a professional.

INSTRUCTIONAL DESIGN TOOL EXCHANGE CONFERENCE
Facilitation prompts for the specialist

INTENT	SUGGESTED REMARKS	ASSUMPTIONS OR GOALS
Set the stage	"It was really great to be in your class today. I enjoyed seeing you in action and seeing your plans unfold with the kids."	Assumes positive presupposition and establishes a fair playing ground.
Begin the reflection	"Can you talk with me a bit about your plan for the lesson? What did you want to accomplish?"	Poses an open-ended question that allows the teacher to take the lead in beginning to talk about his or her learning intention.
Reflect	"Talk with me about what was going on when I was there."	Allows the teacher to talk about his or her emotional reactions, bring up any issues or classroom factors that he/she noticed, etc.
Reflect	"I understand your intent and what happened. To summarize, how do you think it went?"	Encourages the teacher to reflect not only on the goal and what happened, but also the results of the learning design.
Reflect on the data	"As I said before, I really enjoyed being in your class and watching your plans unfold. I was able to complete the Instructional Design Tool. I thought you might like to see what I captured. Are you interested in seeing it?" (Hand the completed copy to the teacher.)	Asks the teacher if he/she is ready to see the data — handing the data to the teacher to begin to analyze.
Reflect on the data	"Talk with me about the information. Reactions or questions? Comments?"	Invites the teacher to react to the data and to question the specialist.
Reflect on the data	"Do you see any relationship between your classroom design indicators and the learning design indicators?"	Invites the teacher to begin connecting the relationship of some of the indicators.

INSTRUCTIONAL DESIGN TOOL EXCHANGE CONFERENCE continued
Facilitation prompts for the specialist

INTENT	SUGGESTED REMARKS	ASSUMPTIONS OR GOALS
Reflect on the data	"Is there anything you notice in your classroom design that you would change to support your learning intent?" "Is there anything you notice in your learning design that has implications for your classroom design?"	Invites the teacher to begin aligning learning needs to the classroom design.
Reflect on the data	"What you see and what you are telling me is _____."	Paraphrases to stimulate the beginning of cause-effect relationship between his or her classroom design and subsequent learning design and accomplishment.
Reflect on the data	"Why do you think that change might cause the improvement to happen?"	Invites analysis.
Plan	"So you are saying that if you _____, then _____."	Invites the teacher to plan and act on his or her own theory, tying together classroom design and learning design.
Plan	"Do you think we should continue using the Instructional Design Tool? Would you like me to come again to look for evidence of the changes you have made?	Invites the teacher to use the tool again to document changes.
Plan	"The next time I'm here, you would like me to _____ while you are _____. Is that right?"	Finalizes the plan.
Reflect on the process	"As you reflect on this process today, tell me in what ways the tool and the exchange conference provided information and support for you."	Reflects on the entire exchange process and determines level of positive feelings for the next time.

■ CONDUCTING THE EXCHANGE

Remember that two of the most important purposes of the exchange conference are to ignite joint curiosity about the teacher's intent and to build a trusting relationship between the participants. The tool is not to be used to pinpoint deficits; rather, it serves as a compilation of what was seen in the room during the designated time. The goal of the exchange is to provide data to encourage the teacher to reflect on his or her "design thinking" and form a future game plan. The teacher's classroom design or learning design will be strengthened through the quality of the exchange and the decisions made in this dialogue.

The exchange conversation will help focus the teacher's curiosity about the relationship between classroom design and learning design, and help the teacher reflect on his or her intent and practice. A teacher may not initially see the relationship between the classroom design and the design's effect on his or her learning goals. Focus the exchange conversation on the relationship of the classroom design indicators to the learning design indicators.

Emphasize not what happened, but what the teacher may have wanted to accomplish and how he or she constructed the learning to accomplish those goals. The comments, questions, and notes sections of the tool may generate the most provocative conversation.

This sequence may be useful in framing the exchange and forging the relationship of the classroom design indicators to the learning design indicators. These suggestions for the exchange conference are a synthesis from Costa & Garmston (2002); Downey et al. (2004); and Garmston & Wellman (1999).

After some reflection, the teacher may be ready to either change some of his or her classroom design or learning design elements. Document these decisions as they will form the "promises" for the next time the specialist observes in the classroom. Use the Instructional Design Tool over time to continue and deepen the conversation about the teacher's design intentionality — thinking overtly about not only the design of the lesson, but the classroom space to support that learning intention.

■ DEVELOPING THEORIES AND MAKING COMMITMENTS

The most important part of the exchange conference is helping the teacher develop a theory about "what might happen if I …" Some teachers may simply want answers, especially those who feel they're falling short of their goals. Teachers are used to being given answers in evaluations or even walk-throughs, so this sense of dependency may be challenging to overcome. Some teachers also may be reluctant to accept or embrace the data as a way to ignite changes.

To frame the conversation so teachers own the data and subsequent changes to their design or behavior, carefully frame questions to provoke thinking and demonstrate respect for the teacher as a professional. Accomplishing both purposes is an art and needs to be practiced. Keep in mind that teachers want to improve and want to make their own professional decisions. Assume positive intent, and even if the exchange conversation does not result in all needed changes, be satisfied with creating a dialogue with the teacher about his or her practice and the plan resulting from the exchange.

When the teacher is ready to think about changes in his or her classroom design and learning design, he or she may wonder out loud by making statements such as "I wonder if I …" or "What do you think would happen if I …" These statements or questions represent the beginnings of a theory of change. If the teacher asks these kinds of questions, reflect the question back instead of accepting it or offering an opinion. Paraphrase or clarify the teacher's theory and ask the teacher if the restated theory is correct, inviting the teacher to hone his or her thinking and solidify a theory of change. Paraphrasing statements may sound like:

- "So you are wondering if you_____, then _____? Is that right?" or
- "What you just said is _____. Do you suspect that a change in _____ might result in_____?"

Toward the end of the exchange conference, the teacher will demonstrate an understanding of his or her proposed change and the impact on students. Ask the teacher to confirm this new theory of change and commit to action. If the result of the exchange is that the teacher invites a return observation to note changes, accept the invitation to return and restate any decisions about changes he or she wants to make in design or practice. Thank the teacher for being open to changes, and confirm any scheduled observations or promised communication. If asked, suggest additional resources to help the teacher plan.

◼ NOTES FOR THE BUILDING LEADER

The Instructional Design Tool may be used with several teachers in a building and, if used more than once with each participating teacher, compiled instructional design data will be useful to the school leaders and members of the school leadership team. Compile and share the data, and facilitate a discussion among the members of the leadership team, asking them to consider if the data from the Instructional Design Tool are compatible with their school improvement efforts.

For instance, data from the tool may reveal that classroom teachers do not routinely create grouping areas in their classrooms, nor do they alter their instructional arrangements. This pattern of classroom and learning design may conflict with the school improvement plan's efforts to foster more differentiation. In this example, the school leadership team's improvement efforts are not supported in practice. Realizing this may lead the team to adjust the school improvement plans or to consider additional professional learning to encourage teachers to create the kinds of classroom and learning designs to support the goal of differentiation.

Use the following questions to guide the Instructional Design Tool data discussion with members of the school improvement team:

- Overall, how are teachers designing their classrooms?
- What kind of classroom arrangements would you see most often in our school?
- How would you summarize the way our teachers design learning experiences?
- How do the results of the Instructional Design Tools align with our school improvement efforts? Are we focusing on classroom design and learning design practices that make a difference?
- How do we need to adjust our plans for professional learning? How should we encourage teachers to adopt promising design practices?
- In what ways have the data from this tool changed our thinking?

CHAPTER

The RESPONSIVE SCHOOL SCAN  T O O L

&
EXCHANGE

As a new school-based instructional specialist, Jack Clark has just been assigned to three comprehensive high schools in his large, urban public school district, and the leaders of all three schools seem eager for his assistance. In learning about the schools, Clark quickly notices significant achievement gaps among diverse groups of students. The high school principals share his concern and have asked Clark to meet with their site-based management teams to discuss how responsive the schools are to the needs of diverse student populations. Clark's goal is to help teachers develop cultural responsiveness and assist them in designing curriculum and instruction that builds on students' diversity rather than targeting student deficits. He realizes the integral part parents and guardians play in promoting high achievement and knows teachers and school leaders will need to capitalize on that strength. He decides to first focus conversation on whether the high schools are designed to promote support, community, and instructional responsiveness. Clark is searching for a tool to begin the dialogue with his site-based management teams.

THE RESPONSIVE SCHOOL SCAN TOOL

School name _____ Date _____

Responsive School Scan Tool team member(s) _____

_____

INDICATORS	🏛	🎯	✒	🚫	NOTES
WELCOMING SCHOOL ENVIRONMENT					
Is there inviting, accurate, and language-appropriate information on the outside school sign?					
Are the school's physical surroundings attractive to visitors and families?					
Is the tone of directions on all exterior entrances high-quality and friendly?					
Are visitors and families greeted and directed to sign in when they first enter the building?					
Are visitors and families warmly and appropriately greeted in the office?					
INFORMATION AND ACCESS					
Do staff in the main office exhibit friendliness, focus, and organization?					
Do visitors and families have a comfortable place to wait in the office?					
Do visitors and families have places near the office or front entrance where they can review information about the school?					
Does the school provide displays or make information readily available for parents to connect with community resources?					
Are the school's mission and vision current and displayed for parents and visitors to see?					
Does the school have a bulletin board on which parents can post announcements or news?					
Does the school have clear and fair processes for families and visitors to access school leaders?					

THE RESPONSIVE SCHOOL SCAN TOOL continued

INDICATORS					NOTES
STUDENT VOICE					
Are quality student work and student achievements displayed throughout the common areas in sensitive and attractive ways?					
Is the purpose of the displayed student work communicated in writing and in appropriate languages?					
Do common areas showcase culturally relevant posters, pictures, or displays?					
Does the media center or teacher resource room contain varieties of culturally responsive materials and resources?					
Do students in common areas demonstrate a sense of focus, purpose, and orderliness?					
CULTURALLY RESPONSIVE CLASSROOMS					
Are the classrooms designed to be intellectually attractive and stimulating to the students?					
Do classrooms include pictures, artifacts, or displays that reflect the students who occupy them?					
Do classrooms include areas for small groups and comfortable places to work and study?					
Does the teacher's classroom appear to be designed for a variety of student groupings?					
Does the teacher use a variety of materials for instruction?					
Has the teacher posted fair and clear procedures for students to view and use to manage their own behavior?					
Does the teacher appear to use fair and equitable management strategies that support student learning and achievement?					

THE RESPONSIVE SCHOOL SCAN TOOL continued

INDICATORS					NOTES
CULTURALLY RESPONSIVE CLASSROOMS continued					
Has the teacher set clear goals for achievement?					
Do displays of classroom work honor and promote high-quality student learning?					
Do students seem engaged in their learning?					
Have teachers capitalized on student interests and/or real-world connections?					

NOTES AND QUESTIONS FOR THE SCHOOL LEADERSHIP

KEY

	Museum quality. There was evidence of extemely high quality.
	Meets the target. The indicator met the operational definition and was on target.
	Needs work. Evidence shows either preliminary or partial effort. Varying and/or inconsistent evidence was noted, and it is recommended that the team construct new efforts to meet this indicator.
	Didn't find it. The indicator was not found to be present at the time of the team visit.

▮ INSIGHTS

Clark may decide to use the Responsive School Scan Tool, which assesses the extent to which a school welcomes diverse parents, guardians, and students who require a new kind of responsiveness to succeed.

Schools that are culturally responsive create an atmosphere where parents and students can achieve and build personal meaning through their own cultural frames of reference. Responsive schools focus on parents' and students' strengths and capacities and have a significant effect on student achievement, according to Joyce Epstein, director of the Center on School, Family, and Community Partnerships and principal investigator for the National Network of Partnership Schools at Johns Hopkins University. Epstein (2005, p. 2) concludes that if schools are intentionally welcoming, involve families, and incorporate systems to focus on students of these families, students achieve more in overall learning, have better attendance, earn more course credits, are more prepared for class, and show other indicators of success in school.

Creating and maintaining a responsive school takes effort. Despite promising research, many schools appear stuck in a deficit model of education in which their leaders perceive parent involvement as meddlesome and students of color and differing ability as deficient. These deficit attitudes prompt leaders to develop schools that have a "no-nonsense, back-to-basics, drill-oriented, dull and uninviting atmosphere where pedagogy is relegated to a monocultural framework, showing a complete lack of preparation for and understanding of the cultural, language, lifestyle, and value differences (the students) will face" (Nieto, 2000, p. 103).

The Responsive School Scan Tool indicates the degree to which a school is adaptive to students' cultures, interests, and instructional needs. Geneva Gay (2000, p. 24) champions a responsive school paradigm where educators focus on removing learning gaps through a design that "teaches to and through" strengths, intellectual capabilities, and prior accomplishments.

Clark, the school-based specialist in the example, believes that this definition of cultural responsiveness can permeate the overall school culture so parents' and students' strengths, interests, and accomplishments are a central focus. Clark is interested in more than how welcoming and attractive schools are. He wants data that will provide an integrated view of how welcoming the climate is and how responsive the school is for students, parents, and guardians. The Responsive School Scan Tool considers a combination of organizational, structural, and pedagogical areas:

- **A welcoming environment:** What efforts have been made to create a welcoming environment for parents, guardians, and students? Do signs, physical surroundings, and communication create a first impression of intentional respect?

- **Information and access:** Can diverse visitors, parents, and guardians access information about the school and community services? Has the school tried to involve parents, guardians, and students in school goals?

- **Student voice:** Do the school's common areas have current, attractive displays of diverse student work and language-appropriate explanations of the works? Do procedures honor students while offering a safe, orderly environment? Do students feel emotionally safe? Are students' diverse perspectives evident in school displays?

- **Culturally responsive classrooms:** Do teachers create attractive classrooms that promote collaboration, communication, and flexibility by adjusting to learning needs? Are students' lives evident in the artifacts and work displayed in interesting and useful ways?

The Responsive School Scan Tool is a three-page inventory that provides 28 indicators of the school's quality in these four organizational, structural, and pedagogical areas. Unlike the other tools, this scan's indicators are designed using this scale: museum quality; meets the target; needs work; or didn't find it. Each indicator records not only effort but also information about the indicators that might need improvement. Observers can use the notes section to document evidence of the indicators and the ending section for general comments or to pose questions for the school leader or leadership team to consider.

■ DECIDING TO USE THE TOOL

Classroom Snapshot Tool (see Chapter 3) results may indicate a need to use the Responsive School Scan Tool to drill down into organizational, pedagogical, and structural issues that may disenfranchise students and families. For example, one school-based specialist used the Classroom Snapshot Tool in 12 to 15 classrooms and found a consistent pattern. These qualities were not found in most classrooms:

- Attractive, rich environment;
- Varieties of materials and resources;
- Respectful tasks for all students;
- Evidence of student engagement in tasks.

The specialist also found wide variation in almost all of the indicators in the classroom snapshot's sections on cultural responsiveness and content design, including:

- Inquiry- and/or experience-based;
- Focus on real-world application;
- Overall culture of fairness and equality;
- Respectful teacher directions;
- Established and fair student routines;
- Teacher capitalization on student interests;
- Teacher-student connections.

Believing that all of these areas may collectively indicate the lack of the school's efforts to systematically create a responsive learning environment, the specialist now may want to use the Responsive School Scan Tool to probe how well the school and staff work intentionally to create a welcoming environment where parents, guardians, and students can flourish and feel connected.

The Responsive School Scan Tool is useful when:

- The results of the Classroom Snapshot Tool show areas of need in structural, organizational, or pedagogical responsiveness;
- The school houses a diverse student and parent population, and school leaders want to examine

Checklist of materials for the Responsive School Scan Tool

- ☐ One copy of the Responsive School Scan Tool to use to compile the data
- ☐ A copy of the Responsive School Scan Tool for each classroom to be observed
- ☐ Clipboard or hard writing surface
- ☐ Extra pencils or pens
- ☐ Timing device or watch
- ☐ School map (optional)

how responsive the school is to its clients;

- Leaders or staff want to examine how teachers are building on the strengths and interests of a diverse group of students in their instruction; or
- The leadership team wants data on how responsive the school is to diverse students and parents.

The Responsive School Scan Tool can be an internal, self-study document to help staff members examine their own perceptions of their responsiveness to parents, guardians, and students. Two ways to use the scan internally are:

- The school leader or leadership team asks teachers and/or staff to complete the Responsive School Scan Tool and bring all completed copies to a meeting to share and discuss, and then the group plans changes to align with school improvement efforts.
- The school principal or assistant principal periodically completes the scan to measure and document efforts to create a more responsive school learning environment.

The scan is also, of course, a useful tool for the specialist to use.

SELECTING PARTICIPANTS

The Responsive School Scan Tool provides data about physical, social, and instructional aspects of the school and requires participants who create a welcoming and effective school learning environment. Office and other staff will be observed during the scan. Randomly selected teachers will be observed to determine how effective and responsive instruction is to the needs of diverse students.

Select teachers who represent the grades and subjects of the school. As with the Classroom Snapshot Tool, select enough teachers so that the compiled results fairly portray the day and time. At least 30% of the teachers in a school constitutes a fair sampling for the pedagogical portions of the scan.

BUILDING TRUST

The Responsive School Scan Tool provides structural, organizational, and pedagogical data showing how sensitive the school is to the needs of its students and parents/guardians. When used properly, the scan sheds light on fundamental, sensitive issues. Therefore, building trust is essential to having an appropriate context for the tool. Be sure to first discuss the scan's purpose with the school leader and talk about where the results may lead. Talk to the staff and be extremely clear that the scan will not be used in any formal evaluation of an individual teacher. Take these additional actions to build trust:

- Talk to building leaders and the leadership team about how they will use the results and the kinds of conversations that may result from using the scan. Be sure that staff members have had foundational professional learning focused on meeting the needs of diverse learners.
- Check that the majority of staff are interested in examining the factors in the scan.
- Share a blank form with teachers and staff before using the scan.
- Discuss the scan's purpose with everyone involved. Tell staff that the focus is on gathering impartial data about how the school creates an equitable, responsive learning environment for parents and students. Share how the school leadership will use the results.
- Point out that the data gathered will reveal only what was found at a specific time on one day.
- Let staff know that completing the scan requires classroom visits.
- Remind the staff that the collective results will be shared with them.

The Responsive School Scan Tool is meant to stimulate dialogue and to spur decision makers to consider ways to create more culturally responsive school and classroom conditions for parents and students. When teachers examine school quality through an equity lens, they may open a provocative dialogue in which participants reflect on their beliefs about racial, economic, gender, and/or lifestyle differences. Some may face uncomfortable truths about their actions.

Teachers and school leaders can have a more powerful conversation about the scan's results if they have had time and opportunity to explore their personal beliefs about equity and how parents, guardians, teachers, and school leaders must work together to provide strengths-based opportunities for all students to be successful.

In *Courageous Conversations About Race* (Corwin Press, 2006), Glenn Singleton and Curtis Linton call these "courageous conversations" and outline ways for participants to have honest dialogue about their personal beliefs, to discuss their responses to disenfranchised students, and to dialogue about how schools create varied achievement rates among groups of students. While they focus on student achievement, Singleton and Linton embrace the important role parents and guardians play in creating a community of success around the school (p. 233).

During these difficult conversations, the usual norms that guide critical dialogue often fall apart as participants discuss disenfranchised parents and students (p. 18). To keep the focus on the school's responsiveness to parents, guardians, and students while allowing participants to be more aware of their own personal beliefs about differing abilities, cultures, languages, races, or philosophies, work strategically with the staff to practice Singleton and Linton's four agreements of courageous conversation:

- Stay engaged.
- Speak your truth.
- Experience discomfort.
- Expect and accept nonclosure.

These four agreements can serve as the norms to provide both security and boundaries for conversations that may ensue before and after using the Responsive School Scan Tool.

USING THE TOOL

The scan requires a thorough walk around the school, including the outside perimeter. First, collect all materials necessary to complete the scan. Allow at least 1½ hours to complete the tool, including time to visit randomly selected classrooms. Approach the school with a visitor's eye, and allow yourself to see all aspects of the school as though it were the first time you were there. Be sure to view all structural, organizational, and pedagogical elements of the school, including the exterior doors, front entrances, the office, the area outside the office, common areas, hallways, classrooms, and classroom walls.

Mark the individual indicators according to the defi-

Practice the indicators

The Responsive School Scan Tool allows for more than a simple yes or no checklist. Study these definitions and practice using the tool before completing an actual scan.

nitions, distinguishing between "museum quality" and "on target." When the evidence is inconsistent or the school seems to have only begun taking action in that area, mark "under construction" to indicate effort that is yet to achieve the standard. If there is no evidence for a particular indicator, then mark "not present."

Make multiple copies of the Responsive School Scan Tool and fill in the "culturally responsive classrooms" indicators for each classroom. Many of these indicators can be observed in five to 10 minutes in a class. Collect all the information and compile the data into one sheet for the school for that day and time. Discard the individual classroom scans so they cannot be used to look for an individual teacher's competence. Then prepare to share the data with the school leader and leadership team.

RESPONSIVE SCHOOL SCAN TOOL INDICATORS

INDICATOR	MUSEUM QUALITY	ON TARGET
WELCOMING SCHOOL ENVIRONMENT		
Is there inviting, accurate, and language-appropriate information on the outside school sign?	School marquee or sign includes accurate, friendly, timely, and language-sensitive information for parents, students, or visitors.	Information on the signage is language-sensitive, accurate, and timely, but not necessarily welcoming to visitors, parents, or students.
Are the school's physical surroundings attractive to visitors and families?	The school's physical surroundings are very well cared for and provide an attractive "walk-up" appeal for the visitor or families.	The surroundings are clean and adequately maintained, yet no additional welcoming or attractive touches are noted.
Is the tone of directions on all exterior entrances high-quality and friendly?	Directions and information are of the highest visual quality and respectfully invite parents and guardians to follow procedures.	The directions and information on the main entrance and most exterior doors are adequate and have a moderately friendly tone.
Are visitors and families greeted and directed to sign in when they first enter the building?	Written greetings are warm, welcoming, and direct families in appropriate languages to sign in at the proper location.	Written greetings direct visitors and families to sign in when they enter the building.
Are visitors and families warmly and appropriately greeted in the office?	Staff immediately and warmly greet visitors or families arriving in the main office.	Office staff appropriately greet visitors and families arriving in the main office.

INDICATOR	MUSEUM QUALITY	ON TARGET
INFORMATION AND ACCESS		
Do staff in the main office exhibit friendliness, focus, and organization?	Office staff seem efficient and use a receptive, friendly, collaborative, problem-solving tone.	The office staff assume their roles with moderate focus and efficiency.
Do visitors and families have a comfortable place to wait in the office?	If visitors and families are asked to wait while in the office, they have an immediately accessible, comfortable place to sit with an adequate number of chairs.	Visitors and families are able to wait in the office in an adequately comfortable area.
Do visitors and families have places near the office or front entrance where they can review information about the school?	The main office or an area in the immediate vicinity provides an attractive, comfortable location for visitors and families to review language-appropriate, current, and pertinent information about the school.	The main office or a nearby area provides a location for visitors and families to review current and pertinent information about the school.
Does the school provide displays or make information readily available for parents to connect with community resources?	A wide range of current, accurate, and language-appropriate flyers and information regarding community resources is available near the front office.	Minimal information about community resources is available near the front office.
Are the school's mission and vision current and displayed for parents and visitors to see?	The current school mission and vision are prominently displayed in appropriate languages.	Either the current mission or vision is displayed in appropriate languages.
Does the school have a bulletin board on which parents can post announcements or news?	An attractive parent corner or prominent location offers parents a place to review specific school announcements or post current information.	Parents can review specific school announcements in a designated location.
Does the school have clear and fair processes for families and visitors to access school leaders?	An efficient procedure, clearly posted in appropriate languages, details how visitors or parents can communicate with school leaders.	The school has a procedure for accessing school leaders.

RESPONSIVE SCHOOL SCAN TOOL INDICATORS continued

INDICATOR	MUSEUM QUALITY	ON TARGET
STUDENT VOICE		
Are quality student work and student achievements displayed throughout the common areas in sensitive and attractive ways?	Current and attractively displayed student work and student achievements decorate many, if not all, common areas and show the work of diverse students.	Current and attractively displayed student work and achievements are exhibited in some of the school's common areas.
Is the purpose of the displayed student work communicated in writing and in appropriate languages?	Descriptions in appropriate languages accompany the student works or accomplishments and explain their purpose.	Descriptions in appropriate languages accompany the student work and some displays explaining their purpose.
Do common areas showcase culturally relevant posters, pictures, or displays?	All common areas showcase culturally relevant pictures, posters, displays, artwork, or motivational information.	Some common areas include culturally relevant pictures, posters, displays, artwork, or motivational information.
Does the media center or teacher resource room contain varieties of culturally responsive materials and resources?	The media center is visually attractive and houses a rich store of culturally relevant and diverse materials.	The media center houses a variety of culturally responsive materials and resources.
Do students in common areas demonstrate a sense of focus, purpose, and orderliness?	Students move efficiently and respectfully in common areas and are managed by student-friendly procedures and personnel.	When appropriate, the students are seen moving adequately through common areas, managed by efficient procedures and personnel.

INDICATOR	MUSEUM QUALITY	ON TARGET
CULTURALLY RESPONSIVE CLASSROOMS		
Are classrooms designed to be intellectually attractive and stimulating to students?	Classrooms are extremely attractive and stimulating to students, containing text and visuals that are age-appropriate and culturally sensitive.	Many classrooms are attractive and stimulating to students, containing text and visuals which are age-appropriate and culturally sensitive.
Do classrooms include pictures, artifacts, or displays that reflect the students who occupy them?	Each observed classroom includes pictures, artifacts, or displays that identify the students' interests, languages, and cultures.	Many classrooms include some pictures or artifacts that identify student interests, languages, and cultures.
Do classrooms include areas for small groups and comfortable places to work and study?	All classrooms include at least one attractive area for either small groups or individual places for students to work or think.	Some classrooms include areas for small groups and individual thinking and/or study.
Does the teacher's classroom appear to be designed for a variety of student groupings?	Each observed classroom's physical layout and organization is designed to accommodate flexible groupings.	Many classrooms appear to be designed for students to be able to work in small groups.
Does the teacher use a variety of materials for instruction?	In all observed classrooms, the teacher uses, or has at his or her disposal, multiple sources of information for students.	In many of the observed classrooms, the teacher uses, or has at his or her disposal, several sources of information for students.
Has the teacher posted fair and clear procedures for students to view and use to manage their own behavior?	Behavior guidelines are prominently posted in each classroom in respectful language.	Many teachers have posted behavior guidelines in respectful language in their classrooms.

RESPONSIVE SCHOOL SCAN TOOL INDICATORS continued

INDICATOR	MUSEUM QUALITY	ON TARGET
CULTURALLY RESPONSIVE CLASSROOMS, continued		
Does the teacher appear to use fair and equitable management strategies that support student learning and achievement?	Teachers use "soft but firm" strategies in managing students. Teachers use respectful language in directing all students through designated tasks.	Many teachers are observed using fair and efficient strategies to manage students.
Has the teacher set clear goals for achievement?	In all classrooms, students can easily see a posted list of the goals for the day's achievement in all appropriate subjects.	Many classrooms include posted goals for student achievement.
Do displays of classroom work honor and promote high-quality student learning?	Student work is posted prominently to promote high achievement. Displays honor students' efforts and reflect all students in the class.	Some student work is posted and high achievement is noted.
Do students seem engaged in their learning?	Almost all students appear to be highly or adequately engaged during the observation time.	Almost all of the students are adequately engaged during the observation time.
Have teachers capitalized on student interests and/or real-world connections?	In most classrooms, the teacher's work and lesson design capitalizes on students' interests or values in the real world. Products or student tasks reflect this intent.	In many classrooms, the teacher's work and lesson design capitalize on student interests or values in the real world.

The exchange

■ PLANNING THE EXCHANGE

The results of the Responsive School Scan Tool are not intended to be used for conferences with individual teachers. The aggregated results of the Responsive School Scan Tool are meant to be compiled to share with the school leadership and leadership team and to be used in school-based analysis and planning. If the scan hasn't been an internal review, plan to debrief with the school leadership team or designees.

This tool is not meant to be used as an equity audit, and results should never be dropped off at the office or in the principal's inbox for leaders to review without a carefully planned exchange conference.

Reflect on the data

In preparing for the exchange with either the leadership or the leadership team, look on the scan for patterns in the data or related indicators. Create a summary of the Responsive School Scan Tool to share with leaders or the leadership team. One way is to shade the cell that indicates the synthesis of your individual scans (see the example). Get a sense of the overall school feel in terms of welcoming atmosphere and responsive instructional climate, write down three to four big ideas that are evident from the tool, and note the connection to the four organizational, structural, and pedagogical areas: a welcoming school environment; information and access; student voice; and culturally responsive classrooms. Narrowing the focus will allow those participating in the exchange to work on a part of the entire school improvement picture and may provide some comfort during the conversation. Also think about what questions group members might pose during the conference. The example on the next three pages may help in preparing for the exchange conference.

RESPONSIVE SCHOOL SCAN TOOL SUMMARY

School name *Leemont Elementary School*   Date *Feb. 8, 2008*

Responsive School Scan Tool team members *Jack Clark — school specialist*

INDICATORS					NOTES
WELCOMING SCHOOL ENVIRONMENT					
Is there inviting, accurate, and language-appropriate information on the outside school sign?	▓				*Marquee – information is up-to-date and in Spanish.*
Are the school's physical surroundings attractive to visitors and families?	▓				*Neat, clean, cheerful and elementary age appropriate.*
Is the tone of directions on all exterior entrances high-quality and friendly?		▓			
Are visitors and families greeted and directed to sign in when they first enter the building?				▓	*Office staff was away – had to wait – no sign for parents to sign in.*
Are visitors and families warmly and appropriately greeted in the office?			▓		*When office staff returned, they were cheerful and focused.*
INFORMATION AND ACCESS					
Do staff in the main office exhibit friendliness, focus, and organization?		▓			*Small circular table and chairs.*
Do visitors and families have a comfortable place to wait in the office?	▓				*Computer workstation where parents could access school web site, materials, pamphlets.*
Do visitors and families have places near the office or front entrance where they can review information about the school?	▓				*District information and some community information.*
Does the school provide displays or make information readily available for parents to connect with community resources?	▓				
Are the school's mission and vision current and displayed for parents and visitors to see?			▓		
Does the school have a bulletin board on which parents can post announcements or news?			▓		
Does the school have clear and fair processes for families and visitors to access school leaders?		▓			

INDICATORS	I	◎	✎	⊘	NOTES
STUDENT VOICE					
Are quality student work and student achievements displayed throughout the common areas in sensitive and attractive ways?		■			*In all hallways there was some student work.*
Is the purpose of the displayed student work communicated in writing and in appropriate languages?			■		*In some cases, there was extensive writing accompanying work — in other cases, the explanation was missing.*
Do common areas showcase culturally relevant posters, pictures, or displays?		■			*There were some commercial posters displayed and some work that demonstrated student cultures.*
Does the media center or teacher resource room contain varieties of culturally responsive materials and resources?		■			*Varieties of resources were noted.*
Do students in common areas demonstrate a sense of focus, purpose, and orderliness?		■			
CULTURALLY RESPONSIVE CLASSROOMS					
Are the classrooms designed to be intellectually attractive and stimulating to the students?			■		*Inconsistently designed classrooms — some visually attractive and stimulating, others not.*
Do classrooms include pictures, artifacts, or displays that reflect the students who occupy them?			■		*No displays or artifacts, pictures that would demonstrate the students and their families.*
Do classrooms include areas for small groups and comfortable places to work and study?			■		*Primary classrooms, yes; intermediate classrooms, no.*
Does the teacher's classroom appear to be designed for a variety of student groupings?				■	*Inconsistent use of groupings in classrooms on day visited.*
Does the teacher use a variety of materials for instruction?			■		*In almost all classrooms, one set of materials or books was being used.*
Has the teacher posted fair and clear procedures for students to view and use to manage their own behavior?		■			
Does the teacher appear to use fair and equitable management strategies that support student learning and achievement?				■	*In some classrooms, students isolated — in almost all of those, the students were of color.*

RESPONSIVE SCHOOL SCAN TOOL SUMMARY continued

INDICATORS					NOTES
CULTURALLY RESPONSIVE CLASSROOMS continued					
Has the teacher set clear goals for achievement?			■		*Inconsistent evidence.*
Do displays of classroom work honor and promote high-quality student learning?			■		*Inconsistent displays — in some classrooms, none.*
Do students seem engaged in their learning?				■	*Varieties of patterns of engagement ranging from highly engaged to rebellious.*
Have teachers capitalized on student interests and/or real-world connections?				■	*Not observed in any classroom.*

NOTES AND QUESTIONS FOR THE SCHOOL LEADERSHIP

KEY

	Museum quality. There was evidence of extemely high quality.
	Meets the target. The indicator met the operational definition and was on target.
	Needs work. Evidence shows either preliminary or partial effort. Varying and/or inconsistent evidence was noted, and it is recommended that the team construct new efforts to meet this indicator.
	Didn't find it. The indicator was not found to be present at the time of the team visit.

■ CONDUCTING THE EXCHANGE

Conduct the exchange conference in a way that honors the work the school has already done and doesn't blame or shame school leaders or the school leadership team. The school may have looked for ways to be more inclusive to parents and equitable for its students, and the Responsive School Scan Tool is a positive step in recognizing the work toward accomplishing this goal. Examining the way schools respond to parents and diverse students is often provocative and upsetting to those involved as participants honestly examine the effects of their intentional and unintentional efforts. Maintain a warm, personal, and positive tone, yet gently prompt the group when it seems members are exploring the issues superficially.

The goal of the exchange is to have the leadership team or school leader leave with a preliminary plan for changes to address some of the indicators from the scan. However, the team may not be able to develop even a preliminary plan during a single exchange conference. Balance reflection and action orientation, and schedule a follow-up exchange if necessary. Be comfortable with this uncertainty, and recognize that exploring issues of responsiveness, equity, and diversity are often grounded in very personal feelings — a fact that can stall action. Allowing group members to fully explore individual and group philosophies behind the data will help them as they commit to improve and build trust in one another.

As group members explore their personal beliefs, encourage them to share their personal theories of schooling

Tips for an exchange with the leadership team

Consider using these facilitation prompts on the next two pages and leading questions for the exchange.

These suggestions for the exchange conference are a synthesis from Costa & Garmston (2002), Downey et al. (2004), and Garmston & Wellman (1999).

and the role of parents and guardians in student achievement. Listen for reactions to the data from the scan, and seize opportunities to have them begin to propose theories of change that may help parents and guardians feel more welcome and students be more successful and included. While the scan is not intended to spark widespread changes in instructional strategy, it does offer indicators of instructional quality through an equity lens.

As group members identify ideas, document their suggested changes. The group may identify more improvements than members can effectively monitor. Use chart paper or a wipe-off board to categorize suggested changes into the four areas and help members focus on a manageable number, then prioritize. In many cases, the elements of change may be incorporated into the school's existing improvement plan.

RESPONSIVE SCHOOL SCAN TOOL EXCHANGE CONFERENCE
Facilitation prompts for the specialist

INTENT	SUGGESTED REMARKS	ASSUMPTIONS OR GOALS
Set the stage	"I really enjoyed being in your school on _____."	Assume positive interest in the results of the scan and establish a fair playing ground.
Set the stage	"You will remember what I was doing and why. You were interested in looking at your school to see if your school was responsive in how it is structured, organized, and managed, and how the teaching supports equitable student learning."	Reflect on the purpose of the Responsive School Scan Tool and leaders' goals for the scan.
Begin the reflection	"Talk about your efforts so far in creating a responsive, equitable, inviting environment. What successes have you already had?"	Pose an open-ended question that allows the school administrators or leadership team to take the lead. Assume positive intent.
Reflect	"Think about those efforts. Have you gotten the results you wanted? Why or why not?"	Reflect on their efforts and gauge what still needs to be done.
Reflect on the data	"Are you interested in seeing the Responsive School Scan Tool information?"	Ask administrators and leaders for permission to review the data with them and begin the process of transferring ownership of the data to the school leaders.
Reflect on the data	"What surprises you? What doesn't?"	Ask the administrators and leaders to put the data in their own context of expectations and individual perceptions.
Reflect on the data	"What patterns do you see?"	Ask participants to begin to synthesize and make sense of the data.
Reflect on the data	"What does the scan reveal overall?"	Summarize the results of the scan.
Reflect on the data	"How does everyone feel about this? What are your reactions? Why do you have these reactions?"	Respond to the data through a personal and professional lens.

Facilitation prompts for the specialist

INTENT	SUGGESTED REMARKS	ASSUMPTIONS OR GOALS
Reflect on the data	"So what you are seeing and what you are telling me is _____."	Paraphrase to stimulate the idea of cause-effect relationship between the indicators and create a responsive environment.
Reflect on the data	"Why do you think that might be so?"	Invite analysis.
Plan	"What would make a difference?"	Invite analysis and move close to a theory of change.
Plan and develop theories	"So you are saying that if, as a team, you devoted efforts to _____, then _____?"	Invite leaders to plan and act on their own theory and paraphrase to get clarity.
Plan and act	"What actions do you think would move you toward accomplishing your theory?"	Urge the team to solidify actions designed to improve the school's structural, organizational, or pedagogical responsiveness.
Plan and evaluate	"How would you want to assess whether your efforts have made a difference?"	Move the team to think about measuring its progress.
Plan and evaluate	"So should we use the scan again to measure that progress? When? And how?"	Ask the team to determine whether the scan should be used again and how — either with an external observer or as an internal self-study.
Reflect on the process	"What did you learn through this? What are you still wondering about?"	Reflect and put the data into perspective.
Commit to change	"How can this information be shared, and what can we do to solidify these improvements?"	Relate the group learning to school improvement.

National Staff Development Council

■ DEVELOPING THEORIES AND MAKING COMMITMENTS

Participants in the exchange conference may propose actions they believe will create a more inviting, responsive, equitable school for parents and students. Listen for theories by responding to and paraphrasing participants' ideas. Document participants' ideas during the exchange using chart paper, a wipe-off board, or some means to compile suggestions. As group members offer their thoughts and ideas, use any opportunity to compare their ideas to existing plans for school improvement so participants are encouraged to check for alignment or conflict. Work to prioritize actions if the scan revealed multiple areas of need and participants are overwhelmed.

If it seems that participants may not be ready to take action but may need to further explore their personal beliefs, suggest that they spend more time preparing before outlining actions. Without a foundation that supports the ideal of equity, any plans would be short-lived and have little impact. If the group needs more time before moving to action, capture the discussion and schedule another meeting. An important component of the exchange conference is to have participants reflect and respond to the proposed changes and discuss how they can communicate the results to their colleagues.

After the exchange conference, meet with all faculty to share the scan's results and any proposed changes. This transparency — sharing the tool, results, and actions — will help build trust among the staff and forge stronger commitments to the recommended changes.

■ NOTES FOR THE BUILDING LEADER

During the exchange conference, participants are more likely to focus on improving if they feel honored for their existing practices, so resist the natural tendency to look only at the "not present" or "under construction" indicators. Build on what already is in place by pointing out what is on target, and focus the conversation on positive ways for the teacher to enhance his or her practice. As with the other tools, try to align new ideas and actions from the exchange conference with existing school improvement plans so teachers don't have that "layering on" feeling when faced with so many areas to improve.

In addition, use the Responsive School Scan Tool as an ongoing way to gauge progress toward creating a more welcoming, responsive environment for parents, guardians, and students. Use the periodic results, whether completed internally by school staff or externally by the specialist, in regular school improvement meetings and to create improvement action plans.

CHAPTER

7

The INSTRUCTIONAL MANAGEMENT T O O L & EXCHANGE

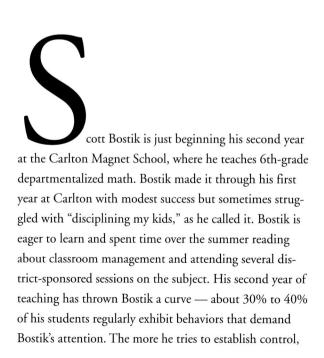

Scott Bostik is just beginning his second year at the Carlton Magnet School, where he teaches 6th-grade departmentalized math. Bostik made it through his first year at Carlton with modest success but sometimes struggled with "disciplining my kids," as he called it. Bostik is eager to learn and spent time over the summer reading about classroom management and attending several district-sponsored sessions on the subject. His second year of teaching has thrown Bostik a curve — about 30% to 40% of his students regularly exhibit behaviors that demand Bostik's attention. The more he tries to establish control,

he feels, the less his students respond to his instruction. Bostik is worried that he is losing the relationship he wants with his students. He seeks out Amanda Altamirano, the school-based specialist assigned to the school, and asks her to drop in to see what is happening in his room.

When the specialist makes an unannounced visit midweek, she finds Bostik working with a small group in front of the room while others have assigned seat work. Bostik seems stiff and rather formal with the students, and the students are not responding enthusiastically. In addition, the other students talk out of turn or are off task, and many have quietly "checked out." Altamirano senses Bostik's frustrations and wishes she had a tool that would begin to add structure to their conversation and help Bostik figure out what to address.

THE INSTRUCTIONAL MANAGEMENT TOOL

Teacher's name _____ School _____ Date/time _____

Grade level/subject _____ Completed by _____

TEACHER DESIGN INTENTIONALITY	YES	NO	?
PHYSICAL SPACE			
The classroom arrangement supports ease of movement.			
Classroom design promotes flexible use of space and groupings.			
Materials are easily accessible to students.			
CLASS GUIDELINES			
Clear visuals indicate class rules and/or expectations.			
The teacher has posted daily learning goals for students to see.			
CLASSROOM CLIMATE			
Student work is displayed to model excellence.			
The environment is attractive and student-centered.			
The classroom shows evidence of student voice and culture.			
INSTRUCTIONAL DESIGN			
Students experience differentiation and/or choices.			
The teacher includes novelty or emotion in instruction.			
Instruction relates to students' lives or interests.			

TEACHER DELIVERY	YES	NO	?
THE TEACHER:			
Frequently uses established procedures.			
Consistently asks students to adhere to rules.			
Clearly states directions and requirements.			
Is both firm and soft in delivering requests.			
Uses proximity and/or touch.			
Intervenes appropriately to manage student behavior.			
Uses positive reinforcement.			
Varies voice in tone and volume.			
Uses appropriate nonverbal signs to manage behavior.			
Seeks students' ideas, thoughts, and/or opinions.			
Effectively balances between teacher instruction and practice.			

THE INSTRUCTIONAL MANAGEMENT TOOL continued

ROUTINE TRANSITIONS		
TRANSITION DESCRIPTION	TIME	STUDENT COMPLIANCE

STUDENT ATTENTION TO REQUESTS IN TERMS OF:
SUITABLE, APPROPRIATE STUDENT MOVEMENT DURING ACTIVITIES:
FOLLOWING DIRECTIONS:
EVIDENCE OF STUDENT ENGAGEMENT:

QUESTIONS FOR THE EXCHANGE

■ INSIGHTS

Bostik enjoys teaching. He chose the profession because he cares about students and believes he has the skills to help them succeed. Altamirano wants Bostik to not only hone his instructional expertise, but also practice how he orchestrates the learning process in his classroom. She is concerned that Bostik appears to be losing his enthusiasm for teaching along with his desire to sustain strong relationships with his students.

Altamirano feels the same way when she observes many new and experienced teachers struggling with instructional management. She is frequently confused about what to do or how to assist teachers as they think about managing the learning in their classrooms.

Bostik's affinity for students and his desire to make a difference propelled him into the field. He is interested in helping students learn, and, from the beginning, his focus was on teaching the *content* of his classes. But as Rick Smith (2001) states, "We may have gotten into the teaching profession to teach science, music, or foreign language, but pretty soon we discover that, in reality, we are in the profession to teach *people*" (p. 11). In addition, Smith points out that many teachers should avoid simply "teach[ing] behavior quickly to get it out of the way in order to teach the content. Behavior is the good stuff. Students need to learn what's appropriate, what's not appropriate, how to tell the difference, and how to discipline themselves to make nurturing choices" (p. 12).

Teachers must teach content and behavior, and if students are to succeed, teachers must see goals for student behavior as inextricably connected to their teaching goals (Smith, 2001, p. 13). Therefore, any discipline dilemma must take into account ways to know and engage students, plan and deliver instruction, and manage their behavior. Compiling the best of what is known about effective classroom management and learning, Robert Marzano (2003a) underscored the components of a successful plan to simultaneously focus on management of powerful learning, rules and procedures, interventions, relationships, student responsibility, and the teacher's mindfulness or mindset.

Student behavior is the core of many teachers' anguish and consternation. Richard Curwin, Allen Mendler, and Brian Mendler (2008) are all too aware of the classroom management dilemma — teachers' confusion and paralysis over the need for consistency, the desire to build relationships with students, and the goal of powerful instruction and learning (p. 33). They say that when focusing on classroom management, teachers typically group students into three categories and say classrooms include these groups in varying proportions:

- Students who rarely break the rules or violate principles;
- Students who break rules somewhat regularly; and
- Students who are chronic rule breakers and generally out of control most of the time.

A good discipline plan controls the student who breaks rules somewhat regularly without overly regulating the majority of students who rarely break rules and without backing into a corner the small percentage of students who are chronic misbehavers (Curwin, Mendler, & Mendler, 2008, p. 33).

Curwin and his co-authors (p. 47) describe three interrelated dimensions to creating an effective plan:

1. The prevention dimension:
- Know and express yourself clearly.
- Know your students.
- Make your classroom motivating.
- Teach responsibility and caring.
- Establish effective rules and consequences.
- Keep yourself current.
- Deal with stressful conflict.

2. The action dimension:
- Stop the misbehavior quickly.
- Get back to great teaching.
- Keep students in class.
- Implement consequences.
- Collect data.

3. The resolution dimension:
- Find what is needed to prevent another problem.

National Staff Development Council

■ DECIDING TO USE THE TOOL

Use the Instructional Management Tool in one or more of the following instances:

- The Classroom Snapshot Tool (see Chapter 3) reveals concerns related to instructional management or student behavior;
- The Instructional Design Tool (see Chapter 5) reveals a need to improve the teacher's ability to design lessons that capture student interest and sustain positive behavior;
- The Engagement Visit Tool (see Chapter 4) points to student behaviors that might lead to issues in instructional management;
- The school leadership team wants schoolwide evidence of instructional management;
- The school leader would like information about new and beginning teachers' abilities to manage instruction;
- A marked increase in discipline referrals points to instructional management issues; or
- School leaders want to initiate a dialogue about the relationship between teachers' instructional intention and classroom management.

Checklist of materials for the Instructional Management Tool

- ☐ One tool for each selected teacher
- ☐ Operational definitions (if desired)
- ☐ Clipboard or hard writing surface
- ☐ Extra pencils or pens
- ☐ Timing device or watch
- ☐ Class photos or roster (optional)

- Develop a mutually agreeable plan.
- Implement the plan.
- Monitor the plan/revise if necessary.
- Use creative/unconventional approaches when necessary.

Scott Bostik is experiencing a kind of instructional management paralysis. At a critical juncture in his career, he is feeling less and less empowered to teach his students and feels instructionally impotent. He is so concerned about students' behavior that his teaching feels less and less effective. Bostik and Altamirano will find the Instructional Management Tool useful as they work together.

The Instructional Management Tool focuses on four aspects of instructional management:

- **The teacher's intended instructional design.** How has the teacher designed the learning space? Are class guidelines posted and are learning goals clearly viewable? Is the classroom climate supportive? Is the environment student-friendly? Is the instruction designed to motivate and engage students?
- **The teacher's delivery.** How is the teacher delivering instruction? How does the teacher involve students in their learning? How is the teacher managing student behavior?
- **Transitions and compliance.** How long is each transition? How well do students comply with the teacher's transition requests?
- **Student responsiveness.** In what ways did the students respond to the teacher's requests, and how well do they know classroom rules and procedures? Did students move around the room appropriately without disrupting instruction? Did students generally follow

the teacher's directions and procedures? Did students seem engaged?

The Instructional Management Tool can capture all four aspects in one short classroom visit and a subsequent time for reflection. The results of the tool enable teachers to build personal theories of what might work better to more consistently engage students and sustain their learning. In addition, by using the tool, teachers see the relationship between instruction and discipline and find ways to manage student behavior while redirecting disengaged students.

SELECTING PARTICIPANTS

Most teachers view instructional management as discipline, and they may be particularly sensitive to concerns about how they manage student behavior. They may be even more overwhelmed when asked to relate management issues to issues of instructional design. For these reasons, participation in the Instructional Management Tool should be, in most cases, voluntary.

Two categories of teachers will especially benefit from the tool. Beginning teachers and teachers new to the school often ask for help with instructional management, and this tool or a portion of it may begin to build teacher awareness of the interrelated components of instruction and management. In addition, teachers whose results on the Instructional Design Tool indicate that they may be struggling with specific student management issues can learn from the data revealed by this tool. The Instructional Management Tool will provide information showing the relationship between the teacher's design and delivery and students' responsiveness and behavior. The Instructional Management Tool also allows the specialist to observe how new, beginning, and veteran teachers manage student transitions, times that often are the playground for disciplinary troubles and loss of focus or control.

The Instructional Management Tool is also useful schoolwide. Aggregated data from several teachers will reveal the state of instructional management in a school and create an information bridge from classrooms to a school profile, providing a focus for professional development and/or action.

When using the aggregated data from multiple Instructional Management Tools to spark school improvement conversations with the school leadership team, remember never to share individual instructional management teacher data with team members, and the results of this tool should never be used for teacher evaluation. The tool's success depends on trust between specialist and teacher, and the specialist's ability to not only observe instructional management but to facilitate and deepen the teacher's understanding of effective learning and management through analysis and theory building.

BUILDING TRUST

Teachers may want help in instructional management but still be reluctant to allow an observer into the room. Although the tool is a just record of what was either observed or not observed along with a time study of transitions, the teacher may look at it as a discipline audit. Reinforce that the tool only gives a glimpse of various factors to provide ideas for a subsequent conversation. Let the teacher know the data are meant to result in a thoughtful inquiry into practice, and that the tool's design is meant to help the teacher focus on one or more aspects of instructional management, as well as see the relationship among all four factors.

Build trust by attending to these questions before using the Instructional Management Tool:

- Are the selected teachers eager to improve their instructional management?
- Have the selected teachers seen a blank tool?
- Have the selected teachers reviewed the operational definitions of each indicator on the tool?
- Do participating teachers know the general time frame for the classrooms visits?
- How will members of the school leadership team be kept informed?
- Do school leaders understand that they will not see

individual results of the Instructional Management Tool?

• Is there a plan for school leaders or members of the leadership team to see aggregated results?

◼ USING THE TOOL

Become familiar with the five parts of the Instructional Management Tool.

• Components 1 and 2 are simple checklists with columns to identify if the indicator was seen or if the specialist has a question. Many of the checklist items require careful observation. For example, the teacher delivery indicators ask how the teacher verbally and nonverbally orchestrates student learning.

• Component 3 is a blank grid for documenting transition times and the degree to which students complied with the teacher's directions.

• Component 4 provides space for reflections and observations about how students responded, moved, followed directions, and about overall student engagement.

• Component 5 is for questions or unresolved concepts to explore with the teacher at the exchange conference in the central section on the tool.

Some of the tool's indicators address teacher design intentionality and may be completed any time during the visit. Practice using the tool in willing teachers' classrooms to become familiar with all of its components. At first, complete only portions in order to become completely familiar with the indicators.

INSTRUCTIONAL MANAGEMENT TOOL INDICATORS

FIRST COMPONENT Teacher design intentionality grid

INDICATOR	OPERATIONAL DEFINITION
PHYSICAL SPACE	
The classroom arrangement supports ease of movement.	The room is arranged in ways that allow students to move quickly and efficiently from large to small groups, individual work, and flexible groups.
Classroom design promotes flexible use of space and groupings.	The room arrangement supports various student groupings for instruction. There is enough open space for students and teacher to move efficiently.
Materials are easily accessible to students.	Teacher and students can easily and efficiently access the various materials.
CLASS GUIDELINES	
Clear visuals indicate class rules and/or expectations.	Desired social or management behaviors are posted in the classroom and are easily readable.
The teacher has posted daily learning goals for students to see.	Students can clearly see the day's specific learning objectives, i.e. "what we are going to accomplish today."
CLASSROOM CLIMATE	
Student work is displayed to model excellence.	Various examples of student work are displayed in the classroom, and all examples are of superior quality.
The environment is attractive and student-centered.	The classroom has attractive displays and is created to be student-centered. Rich print and visuals are used to stimulate learning.
The classroom shows evidence of student voice and culture.	Student artifacts indicate the culture and interests of the students who inhabit the classroom.
INSTRUCTIONAL DESIGN	
Students experience differentiation and/or choices.	The instruction is differentiated in terms of what the student should know or be able to do, the kinds of activities asked of the student, or how the student will demonstrate proficiency.
The teacher includes novelty or emotion in instruction.	Use of humor, inquiry, surprise, or novelty is evident in the instruction.
Instruction relates to students' lives or interests.	The teacher's design includes the connection of the concept or skill to application in students' lives or their personal interests.

INSTRUCTIONAL MANAGEMENT TOOL INDICATORS continued

SECOND COMPONENT Teacher delivery grid

INDICATOR	OPERATIONAL DEFINITION
THE TEACHER:	
Frequently uses established procedures.	The teacher efficiently manages learning by using procedures the class has practiced.
Consistently asks students to adhere to the rules.	The teacher frequently reminds students of his or her expectations and adheres to the expectations.
Clearly states directions and requirements.	The teacher's directions and spoken guidelines are clear and give boundaries to the assignment or direction.
Is both firm and soft in delivering requests.	When managing the instruction, the teacher's language is clear but delivered in a way that is consistent, calm, and nonabrasive.
Uses proximity and/or touch.	The teacher comes within one arm's reach of the targeted student or touches the student in an intentional and supportive manner.
Intervenes appropriately to manage student behavior.	The teacher efficiently and quickly intervenes to stop undesired student behavior and redirect the student.
Uses positive reinforcement.	The teacher warmly and personally acknowledges students' efforts in a positive, supportive way.
Varies voice in tone and volume.	The teacher varies his or her voice throughout the teaching segment, using it as an instrument to engage students.
Uses appropriate nonverbal signs to manage behavior.	The teacher uses nonverbal signals such as nods, eye contact, or gesture to redirect students' behavior.
Seeks students' ideas, thoughts, and/or opinions.	The teacher probes and questions to spark inquiry or to attach personal interest to the activity or task.
Effectively balances between teacher instruction and practice.	The teacher mixes directed instruction and student practice to keep students attentive and engaged.

INSTRUCTIONAL MANAGEMENT TOOL INDICATORS continued

THIRD COMPONENT Routine transitions and compliance time series

Carefully document transitions between activities or from a "teach piece" to a "practice" segment in the lesson and note how long the transition takes, as well as any evidence of how well students complied with the transition request. Time how long it takes the majority of the students (at least 80%) to comply, and note under "student compliance" students who did not comply within the majority time. Mark every transition that takes place during the observation. For example:

TRANSITION DESCRIPTION	TIME	STUDENT COMPLIANCE
Change from math whole-group instruction to guided practice — teacher requested that students get materials out and begin to prepare paper to practice five problems put on the screen.	4 minutes	Four students moved very slowly to get their paper and pencils out. At the end of four minutes, these four students were still getting organized.
Request by the teacher to stop working on the five problems at their desks and look to the screen for troubleshooting.	1 minute	Students quickly stopped their work or completed the problem and waited for the teacher's instruction. Many students were not finished with all five problems.
Teacher added five more problems to the screen after the troubleshooting sequence and asked students to finish all 10 problems.	1 minute	Five students did not immediately return to individual work. One began doodling, one began reading a book quietly underneath the table, and three went to the teacher for individual help. The teacher was unable to quickly scan the room to see if all others were compliant.

FOURTH COMPONENT Reflection on student responsiveness

This component is best completed after the actual classroom visit. Review all the recorded data, and use the data to register a "balcony" view of how students responded to the teacher's design, delivery, and requests. This section is an important part of finishing the picture of instructional management, and since it will help the specialist coalesce his or her thoughts for the exchange conference, should be completed prior to the conference.
Complete the fourth component in terms of:

- Suitable, appropriate student movement during activities: Summarize any and all student movement during the classroom visit.

- Following directions: Detail any evidence of students quickly following directions and report any patterns of disruption.

- Evidence of student engagement: Note when students make eye contact, are obviously enthusiastic about the task, and generally stay on task for the time specified by the teacher.

INSTRUCTIONAL MANAGEMENT TOOL INDICATORS continued
FIFTH COMPONENT Provocative, open-ended reflections and questions

The fifth component in the tool is the blank cell in the middle of the design. Use this space to synthesize the information and look for broad underlying questions that might spark discussion during the exchange conference.

Write "wonderings," but avoid filling in suggestions.

Some students may become quite disruptive when an observer is in the classroom using the tool. In these cases, consider studying only one portion of what is happening, such as the student behavior or the teacher delivery. Sometimes disruptive students dominate the climate and outcomes of the teaching segment to such an extent that the tool simply should not be completed as intended.

Conduct the exchange conference just about the disruptive students or using the completed components. The tool's usefulness depends on the classroom context and the moment of observation.

The exchange

PLANNING THE EXCHANGE

When planning the exchange, examine the completed Instructional Management Tool for indicator relationships, and try to paint a general data portrait of what happened during the observed instruction. The completed tool will reveal a pattern from similar strands in more than one component. While it is impossible to list every pattern, these are the most typical:

Pattern #1: "My classroom is not arranged to support my instruction." The classroom is too crowded to support easy movement. Materials are hard to access, and the teacher is not able to use proximity or touch to direct student behavior. Students spend too much time in transition because it's difficult to move, and the class loses valuable instructional time as well as interest in the activity.

Pattern #2: "I'm inconsistent in my expectations and actions." The teacher has posted class guidelines and learning goals, but doesn't consistently use the procedures and does not always adhere to her own guidelines. The teacher may use ineffective interventions rather than positive reinforcement. When giving directions for transitions, the teacher does not consistently command compliance; consequently, some students are not consistently engaged.

Pattern #3: "What I have designed and delivered isn't

Tips for the exchange conference

This sequence on the next three pages may provide broad suggestions for the exchange conference.

engaging." The teacher has created a whole-group teaching segment, but concentrates so much time on delivery that students lose interest before practicing the new skill. The transition from lesson to practice is not energizing, and unfocused behavior causes lost practice time. Students appear bored, and at least one-third of them are observed to be off task during the practice segment.

Some general questions may help in preparing for the exchange conference:

- Does the completed tool paint a portrait of the teacher's instructional management? Describe it.
- What surprises did the tool yield? What patterns?
- How will the teacher be likely to react to the data? How would the teacher explain the observations from that period?
- What questions might the teacher have after reviewing the completed tool?
- What did the transition analysis reveal about the teacher's instructional management?
- What relationships are evident among indicators in different components?
- What do you hope the teacher gains from analyzing the completed tool?

Carefully review the completed tool to uncover relationships among the teacher's design, delivery, and resultant student behavior. Use the results as a catalyst for discussion at the conference.

INSTRUCTIONAL MANAGEMENT TOOL EXCHANGE CONFERENCE
Facilitation prompts for the specialist

INTENT	SUGGESTED REMARKS	ASSUMPTIONS OR GOALS
Set the stage	"It was really great to be in your class today. I enjoyed seeing you in action and seeing your plans unfold with the kids."	Assume positive presupposition and establish a fair playing ground.
Begin the reflection	"Please visit with me a little about the way you have organized the classroom. How does this physical space help your instruction?"	Pose an open-ended question that allows the teacher to take the lead in talking about his or her classroom design.
Reflect	"You seemed to have real purpose to your lesson. Can you tell me about it?"	Provide the teacher time to talk about the lesson and what he or she wanted to accomplish.
Reflect	"I understand your intent and what happened. To summarize, how do you think it went?"	Encourage the teacher to reflect not only on the goal and what happened but also the results of the learning design.
Invite the teacher to review the data	"You will remember that we were working on your instructional management. You might think of that as discipline, but it's really much more than that. I was so glad to be in your classroom and was able to use the Instructional Management Tool to capture some interesting information about not only your learning design, but also how the students responded. Should we look at it?"	Remind the teacher of the tool's intent and invite him or her to look at the results.
Reflect on the data	"Let's walk through the tool and, as we do, please talk to me about indicators that you think were related to each other or patterns you see."	Invite the teacher to react to the data and to pose questions.

Facilitation prompts for the specialist

INTENT	SUGGESTED REMARKS	ASSUMPTIONS OR GOALS
Reflect on the data	"What jumps out at you? Are there some aspects to the tool that you see as related? What are they?"	Ask the teacher to make broad connections.
Reflect on the data	"Let's go through all components of the tool. What would have to change in your learning design to support the goals you had for your instruction?"	Invite the teacher to begin to align learning needs to the classroom design.
Reflect on the data	"Talk to me about your delivery. Did anything here surprise you?"	Invite the teacher to begin to think about his or her own behavior in relation to the students.
Reflect on the data	"Let me describe the transitions and what I saw. What do you think about that? What are your immediate reactions?"	Invite the teacher to mentally run through the transitions and speculate about them.
Reflect on the data	"Now let's look at student responsiveness. What are your thoughts?"	Invite the teacher to look at the results of both his or her actions and learning design, and the way students responded.
Reflect on the data	"What do you make of this? Can you put all of the pieces together for me? What do you think?"	Invite the teacher to begin to connect the components in terms of instructional management.

INSTRUCTIONAL MANAGEMENT TOOL EXCHANGE CONFERENCE continued
Facilitation prompts for the specialist

INTENT	SUGGESTED REMARKS	ASSUMPTIONS OR GOALS
Reflect on the data	"What you are seeing and what you are telling me is _____."	Paraphrase to stimulate thinking about cause-effect between learning design, teacher behaviors, and student responsiveness.
Reflect on the data	"Why do you think that might be so?"	Invite analysis.
Plan and develop a theory	"You are saying that if you _____, then _____."	Invite the teacher to plan and act on his or her own theory tying together classroom design and learning design.
Plan	"Do you think we should continue using the Instructional Management Tool? Would you like me to come again to look for evidence of any changes you have made?"	Invite the teacher to use the tool again to document changes.
Plan and confirm the theory	"The next time I'm here, you would like for me to _____ while you are _____."	Finalize the plan.
Reflect on the process	"As you reflect on this process today, what does it do for you?"	Reflect on the exchange process and determine level of positive feelings for the next time.

■ CONDUCTING THE EXCHANGE

In conducting the exchange, remember that the teacher already may have perceptions of his or her classroom management during the observed time and may be dismayed at the observations recorded on the tool. Because of the tool's complexity, carefully walk the teacher through the data, paying particular attention to the teacher's inclination to believe that any "no" markings are areas of deficiency. Point out that the tool indicates only one moment in time in the teacher's instructional management. Focus the conversation on the relationship among the teacher's intended design, behaviors, and resulting student behaviors.

■ DEVELOPING THEORIES AND MAKING COMMITMENTS

The exchange conference teaches educators to take time to develop their own theories of what might work better the next time. Teachers do not often think about their own theories of instruction, but they have them. Theories are the basis for any of the hundreds of decisions they make each day.

In building his or her theory, the teacher must be able to connect the components of the tool and develop a personal game plan about his or her own teaching success — and may need help to make that connection. Guide this theory building by helping the teacher review all of the tool's components and writing out key ideas on a board or chart paper. Help the teacher build a theory by systematically pointing out connections among the design, delivery, and outcomes of the observed teaching segment.

Once the teacher begins to suggest changes and possible resulting positive behavior, use paraphrasing to identify the potential theory:

"OK, you are saying that if you

_____,

then_____.
Am I right on this?"

If the teacher confirms the statement's accuracy, review the theory and its intended outcome. This statement forms the contract for the next visit.

Note: The Instructional Management Tool and Exchange is a great device not only for looking at designs, behaviors, and outcomes, but also for teaching teachers effective instructional management. Talk with teachers about the tool's design indicators, teaching behaviors, transitions, and outcomes to build a holistic view of instructional management. Informal conversations about the tool's structure and components may be just as useful as formal observations and exchanges for teachers who are having management or discipline issues. Share an uncompleted tool and ask teachers to use it as an informal self-assessment as a way to open up productive conversations.

■ NOTES FOR THE BUILDING LEADER

The Instructional Management Tool is intended to be used with individual classroom teachers; however, results from individual observations may be compiled into useful aggregates across the school, departments, or levels. Consider uses for aggregated results by asking:

- What does the tool reveal about teaching and management behaviors across the school?
- Are some teaching transition patterns prevalent, or are there reasons transitions are not as effective?
- Do students in the school generally respond to teachers' instructional designs and teaching delivery? Why or why not?
- Do beginning teachers demonstrate behavioral patterns or design issues that could be addressed through professional development or mentoring?
- Are there connections between schoolwide discipline issues and the aggregated results on the Instructional Management Tool? What are they?
- How would we describe instructional management in the school?
- How would we want to change the management of students? How would we know if our efforts were working?

CHAPTER

The MISSING L I N K

BUILDING SCHOOLWIDE ANALYSIS
FROM INDIVIDUAL IMPROVEMENT

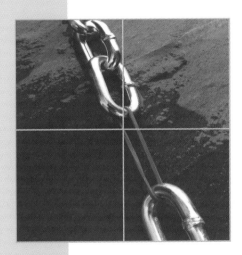

Tools and exchange conferences can give school leaders an easily understandable way to align their work in improving classroom quality to their work in developing the school as a whole through an integrated cycle of analysis, learning, planning, and action. Using the tools requires thoughtful and deliberate design. School leaders create a system in which data from the tools simultaneously provide information about each classroom and paint a picture of school quality. They use the tools to systematically capture benchmark information that helps link professional development efforts with school improvement plans and tests the tools' effects from individual to individual.

Finally, coherence can exist between individual improvement and school improvement. Data from the tools create information bridges between classroom and school improvement. School-based specialists and building leaders use the data and dialogue with individual teachers to connect to the larger structure of school effectiveness.

A critical set of questions, if used often and consistently, drives this integration of individual teacher learning, support, and improving school effectiveness:

- What do students need to learn or be able to do?
- What conditions need to be present in classrooms to support these student goals?
- What does each person need to learn in order to create or sustain these conditions?

- What are the effects of individuals' efforts and school efforts?
- In what ways does each person need to adjust his or her plans?
- Are teachers frequently asking themselves, "What is my plan for learning and action, and in what ways is it a part of the school's professional development plans?"
- How are we, as a school, progressing collectively toward our goals?

The most successful school improvement teams are not satisfied with simply having data. Teams thoughtfully examine the data through a school-level exchange conference to guide discussions and help teachers make decisions about professional learning. Teachers use the tools to build possible improvement theories, plan for success, and benchmark and gauge progress in their efforts.

Data from the five tools may be aggregated into diagnostic summaries that leaders and site-based advisory teams can use to focus professional learning and resources and to accelerate the improvement process. Data from the tools can be aggregated, displayed, and shared with a number of interested groups in the school, from the school improvement team to the entire faculty.

Looking at classroom and school improvement simultaneously can offer distinct benefits. Using tools with individual teachers yields results one classroom at a time, but when the specialist or school leader looks at practices schoolwide, a multifaceted picture emerges of how well individual teachers' improvement efforts are aligning with others and of areas of excellence or issues.

Systematic, thoughtful use of the five tools will help educators create powerful job-embedded professional learning that:
- Focuses on side-by-side collaboration with colleagues;
- Builds on people's strengths and natural curiosity;
- Uses tools to gather information and build on teachers' natural desire to improve;
- Uses collective data to build information bridges from classroom improvements to school improvement;

- Creates moment-in-time data pictures of school progress;
- Facilitates the use of these data pictures by leaders of the school to ignite and sustain planning and evaluation;
- Continues the cycle of inquiry, data gathering, data pictures, development of actions, and knowledge of results.

Using these tools is hard work and requires intense preparation. The tools result in collaborative dialogue about intent, practice, and action and can lead to deeper, more profound conversations for many practitioners. While the tools and exchange conferences are grounded in the philosophy of a relationship-based, collegial collection and exchange, they also hold teachers and the specialist or school leader accountable through the data they reveal. Using the tools data, participants are compelled into a deliberate, actionable conversation about classroom practice and are focused on student results.

The charge

When adult learning goals are directly aligned with student goals, then professional development, strategic use of tools, aggregation of tool data, and exchange conferences continuously frame and hone the conversations about "the effects of our efforts." All of the information revealed from the tools and talk call for new actions or adjusting plans to reach the central focus — the students — and the process continues in a cycle of improvement.

Tools and talk become a mechanism to support information exchanges and create new knowledge, and to support a different way of thinking about data, relationships, and change. The charge for education professionals then, is to maintain the commitment, courage, and strength to build necessary relationships and to use real data to ignite and sustain those focused conversations, leading to solid improvements and building worth among teacher leaders, students, and the families who support them.

CONTINUOUS CYCLE OF IMPROVEMENT

The strategic and continuous use of tools, followed by dialogue and decision making, are a framework for school leaders and school improvement teams.

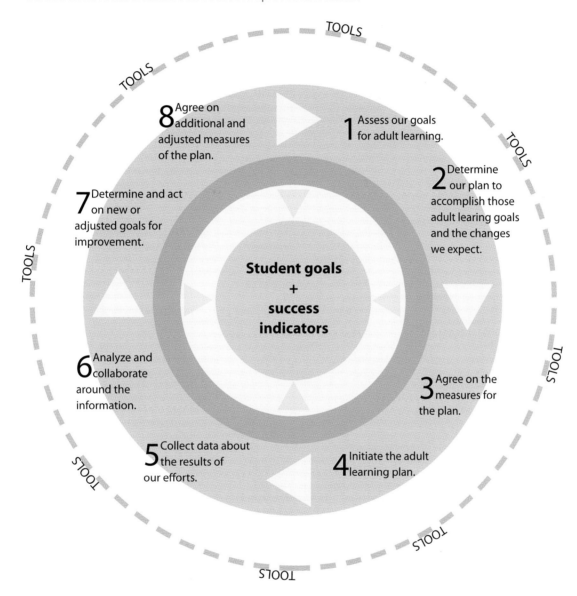

The diagram shows that student goals, the "what do our students need to learn or be able to do," are the core of the integrated improvement process. Once student goals have been determined, adults must analyze their own learning goals to determine how those goals will help accomplish student goals.

BUILDING THE BRIDGE FROM INDIVIDUAL TOOL TO SCHOOLWIDE ANALYSIS

TOOL	DETAIL	INTENDED USE OF THE TOOL	BRIDGE TO SCHOOLWIDE ANALYSIS	SCHOOL IMPROVEMENT TEAM OR WHOLE-FACULTY USE
Classroom Snapshot	Chapter 3	To scan multiple classrooms and gain a sense of classroom quality schoolwide.	Compile multiple classroom scans into a snapshot of that school for the day and time.	• Look at patterns of indicators and detect broad areas for discussion and planning. • Look at indicators to spark dialogue about a vision for the quality of instruction in classrooms. • Use patterns revealed through the classroom snapshot to link to specific tools. • Use patterns to suggest ideas for professional learning. • Use data to adjust or focus school improvement plans.
Engagement Visit	Chapter 4	To examine the relationship between engaging teacher behaviors and student behaviors in individual classrooms.	Use multiple teachers' results for a data picture of schoolwide patterns.	• Look at patterns among indicators and detect broad areas for discussion and planning. • Use patterns to diagnose possible uses of other tools to collect more information. • Use patterns to probe engagement, such as discussing differences among genders, races, etc. • Use patterns to plan professional learning for the school or departments. • Use the data to adjust school improvement plans.
Instructional Design	Chapter 5	To determine the relationship between classroom design and instructional design in a single classroom.	Compile multiple teachers' results to create a data portrait of schoolwide patterns.	• Look at patterns among indicators and detect broad areas for discussion and planning. • Use patterns revealed through the Instructional Design Tool to link to additional tools. • Use patterns to plan professional learning for the school or departments. • Use patterns to consider physical changes to classrooms. • Use standards on the tool to establish schoolwide standards for teachers. • Use the data to adjust or focus school improvement plans.

BUILDING THE BRIDGE FROM INDIVIDUAL TOOL TO SCHOOLWIDE ANALYSIS continued

TOOL	DETAIL	INTENDED USE OF THE TOOL	BRIDGE TO SCHOOLWIDE ANALYSIS	SCHOOL IMPROVEMENT TEAM OR WHOLE-FACULTY USE
Responsive School Scan	Chapter 6	To get a sense of how the entire school encourages parent and student ownership and commitment to the school and learning through looking at multiple classrooms in conjunction with an overall school walk-through.	Create an overall picture of how the school functions as a supported community of learning.	• Look at patterns among indicators and detect broad areas for discussion and planning. • Use patterns to determine use of other tools, such as the Engagement Visit Tool, the Instructional Design Tool, and/or the Instructional Management Tool. • Use patterns to plan professional learning for the school. • Use data to communicate with parents and/or parent advisory teams to build broader support. • Use results to adjust school improvement plans.
Instructional Management	Chapter 7	To analyze individual teachers' management decisions for their effect on instruction.	Compile across multiple teachers to create a data picture of the school and address overall management issues.	• Look at patterns among indicators and detect broad areas for discussion and planning. • Use patterns to diagnose possible uses of other tools, such as the Engagement Visit Tool or the Instructional Design Tool. • Use patterns to plan professional learning for the school. • Compare teacher patterns with school management or discipline records. • Use results to adjust the school improvement plan.

From classsroom to school

School-based specialists or school leaders should study how each tool contributes to a schoolwide portrait of progress and create a plan that merges individual tool results with overall school progress. This chart provides a synopsis of each tool, its intended use, how it can be used for schoolwide analysis, and how the school improvement team or whole faculty can use the aggregated results to discuss changes in practice.

CALENDAR OF LEARNING

One school's story

The narrative at right demonstrates how one school used *Tools & Talk* methods from August 2007 through February 2009 to create the results-based integration of:

See pp. 134-135 for an abbreviated version of this timeline.

- Tools and data;
- Data analysis;
- The exchange conferences;
- The aggregation of data into schoolwide pictures;
- The sharing of data with teams or faculties;
- The ongoing planning using data as benchmarks; and
- The design of professional learning resulting from the tools, the conferences, and school improvement planning decisions.

The example details how the school integrated its system of tools, analysis, professional development, and action, but this particular plan cannot be generalized to every school. Main Street Middle School's school-based specialist, school leaders, and school improvement team used the tools and included data in planning school improvement. Their efforts over 1½ years of planning and implementation is detailed here. Note the schedule markers and integration of tools, analysis, professional development, and actions as staff worked together, both individually and collectively, for better outcomes for students.

August 2007

The school improvement team reviewed the latest student performance information, including state-mandated testing results. Team members matched state student learning standards against recent student performance and target specific mathematics and writing student performance goals. The team presented the goals to the whole faculty, and faculty members determined how they, in their departments, could support the student goals. They also used the classroom snapshot indicators to launch a discussion of and agreement on the classroom quality conditions necessary in all of their classrooms to support student performance. The faculty members helped formulate their overall common adult learning goals that would support student mathematics and writing goals.

August to early October 2007

Once the adult learning goals were targeted, teachers began extended conversations in departmental meetings on how they would like to engage in their own learning. They shared their ideas with the school improvement team, which determined schoolwide designs for professional learning to support goals for improving student achievement in mathematics and writing. School leaders secured the resources and implemented the first components of the professional learning plan.

Early October to early November 2007

Teachers began participating in multiple professional development designs that, at this point, included both training and small study groups in which they periodically examined student work in mathematics and writing. Meanwhile, the school-based specialist met with the school improvement team to discuss overall plans. The team examined the tools and suggested that the school-based specialist share the Instructional Design Tool and the Instructional Management Tool with all teachers in small groups. All teachers were introduced to the two tools and their operational definitions, and were asked which tool they wanted the specialist to use when informally visiting their classrooms. Teachers volunteered for either tool based on individual self-assessments. The two tools were the basis of the specialist's classroom observations for the first part of the school year.

Mid-November 2007 to January 2008

Professional learning continued. The school-based specialist used the Instructional Design Tool or the Instructional Management Tool in teachers' classes and conducted individual exchange conferences. She aggregated the tool data into school profiles without individual teachers' names and worked with the school improvement team in a group exchange conference to analyze indicators from the data. The team used this dialogue, samples of student mathematics and writing work, and informal feedback from departments about student progress to capture benchmark information about members' plans to improve mathematics and writing.

Early January 2008

The specialist continued to use the Instructional Design or Instructional Management Tool with teachers, and the school improvement team asked all teachers to complete an individual survey capturing their perceptions of progress, success, and adjustments needed to achieve student goals. After receiving and compiling the survey information, the improvement team consulted with the principal on mid-course recommendations to further refine professional development plans.

Mid-January 2008

The school improvement team recommended that the school-based specialist use the Classroom Snapshot Tool to capture a sense of overall learning quality. The school-based specialist used the snapshot randomly in 45% of classrooms on one day and compiled the results in a chart in preparation for meeting with the school improvement team.

February 2008

The school-based specialist conducted a group exchange conference with the school improvement team to analyze the results of the classroom snapshot. The team decided to share the results with the whole faculty at the February faculty meeting. Departments analyzed results, celebrated the indicators that were found in most classrooms, dialogued about ways to hold themselves accountable for maintaining those indicators, and had a lively conversation about the indicators, committing to work on

"engaging student tasks" since the specialist had not observed many indicators in this area during the January classroom visits.

Mid-February to March 2008

In three separate faculty meetings, the school improvement team focused on one or more indicators of "engaging student tasks," and faculty members learned how these indicators look in practice. Each department committed to working on one or more specific indicators and to sharing results in subsequent department meetings.

March to May 2008

The school improvement team met to share additional student mathematics and writing work that departments compiled and decided to ask the school leadership team to consult with district officials to plan and conduct training on student engagement in August at the start of the new school year. The specialist continued using the Instructional Design Tool and the Instructional Management Tool. The school improvement team analyzed state-mandated student testing results and found small gains in mathematics and writing. Team members used the information to focus school improvement plans and professional learning designs for mathematics and writing. They committed to continually refining mathematics and writing student goals.

August 2008

District instructional specialists spent a day with the whole faculty for professional development on student engagement. Faculty members were introduced to the Engagement Visit Tool, saw examples of the tool, and studied the tool for use in their classrooms. They dialogued in small groups about how the focus on engagement (pedagogical work) would help them achieve their mathematics and writing goals for students.

September to late November 2008

Teachers continued working on refined mathematics

and writing content strategies and collected student work samples to analyze. Based on widespread interest, the school-based specialist began using the Engagement Visit Tool in all teachers' classrooms and conducted individual exchange conferences with teachers. The specialist aggregated all of the engagement visit data without using individual teacher names and gave departments their own aggregated data for discussion, analysis, and commitment to action.

December 2008

The specialist shared aggregated schoolwide engagement visit data with the school improvement team and facilitated a group exchange conference. The school improvement team shared the schoolwide results at a faculty meeting, and the district officials who led the August professional development engaged in a question-and-answer session with teachers about specific student engagement learning.

January 2009

The school improvement team met and reviewed

mathematics and writing student samples, compared work with previous samples, and considered any additional support needed for a focus on student engagement. The specialist continued to use the Engagement Visit Tool. The school improvement team asked the specialist to conduct another round of classroom snapshot visits to check for overall quality and for data to compare with prior indicators on "engaging student tasks."

February 2009

The school-based specialist conducted another classroom snapshot on one day, including as many of the previous participating teachers as possible. She aggregated the data and shared results with the school improvement team. The data revealed improvements in several indicators, including some in the "engaging student tasks" section of the tool. Team members further defined their focus on engagement as revealed by the tool, looking at progress based on student work samples, informal teacher feedback, and tool aggregated results to adjust adult learning goals.

August 2007	August to early October 2007	Early October to early November 2007	Mid-November 2007 to January 2008	Early January 2008	Mid-January 2008	February 2008

Student goals and indicators of success are established.

Teachers work in departments and vertical teams to develop not only what they will learn but advise the principal on how they feel the learning will best occur within their context. A professional development plan is developed and confirmed by all.

School improvement team meets several times to hear of progress and to see summaries of student work.

Aggregated results of the Classroom Snapshot Tool are exchanged with members of the school improvement team.

Faculty meeting is held to discuss the results of the Classroom Snapshot Tool. Faculty generate specific needs and plans to create more engaging student tasks (revealed by the snapshot).

School improvement team meets to review preliminary professional development evaluative results and to make recommendations.

Teachers agree on common adult learning goals that relate directly to student goals and support classroom conditions.

School improvement team asks for the Classroom Snapshot Tool to be used to check for overall school classroom learning quality.

Teachers consult with each other on classroom conditions that will support their student goals.

Teachers begin working on ways they can promote mathematics learning goals in multiple professional development designs. Evaluative evidence is collected through a variety of means.

Classroom Snapshot Tool is conducted and aggregated for the school improvement team.

Classroom Snapshot Tool review

School study of tools

Use of tools to support teachers

Classroom Snapshot Tool

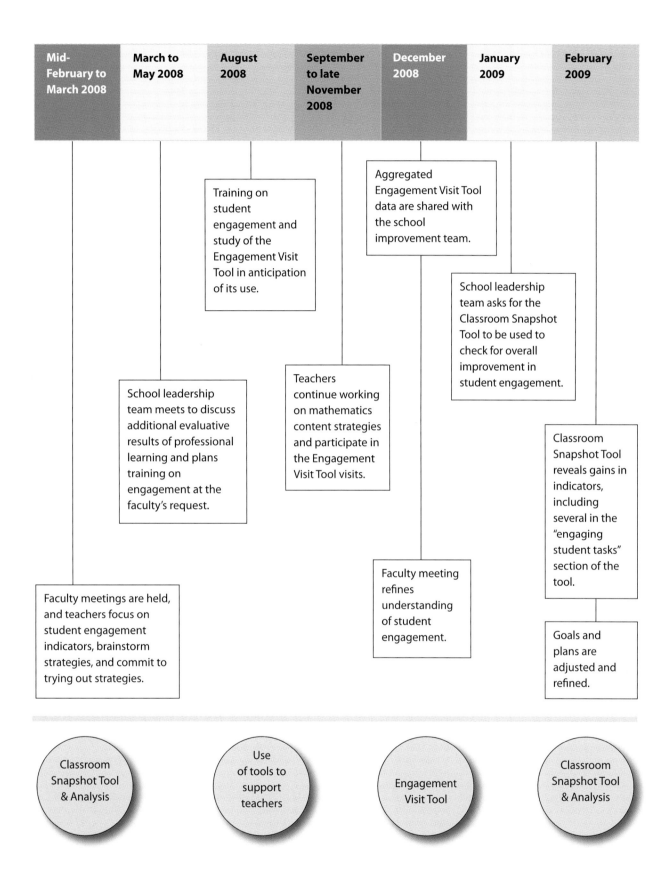

Mid-February to March 2008	March to May 2008	August 2008	September to late November 2008	December 2008	January 2009	February 2009

Training on student engagement and study of the Engagement Visit Tool in anticipation of its use.

Aggregated Engagement Visit Tool data are shared with the school improvement team.

School leadership team asks for the Classroom Snapshot Tool to be used to check for overall improvement in student engagement.

School leadership team meets to discuss additional evaluative results of professional learning and plans training on engagement at the faculty's request.

Teachers continue working on mathematics content strategies and participate in the Engagement Visit Tool visits.

Classroom Snapshot Tool reveals gains in indicators, including several in the "engaging student tasks" section of the tool.

Faculty meetings are held, and teachers focus on student engagement indicators, brainstorm strategies, and commit to trying out strategies.

Faculty meeting refines understanding of student engagement.

Goals and plans are adjusted and refined.

Classroom Snapshot Tool & Analysis

Use of tools to support teachers

Engagement Visit Tool

Classroom Snapshot Tool & Analysis

References

Cantor, J., Kester, D., & Miller, A. (2000, August). *Amazing results! Teacher expectations and student achievement (TESA) follow-up survey of TESA-trained teachers in 45 states and the District of Columbia.* EDRS publication following a presentation at the annual meeting of the California Educational Research Association. (ERIC Document Reproduction Service No. SP039357)

Costa, A.L. & Garmston, R.J. (2002). *Cognitive coaching: A foundation for renaissance schools.* Norwood, MA: Christopher-Gordon.

Curwin, R.L., Mendler, A.N., & Mendler, B.D. (2008). *Discipline with dignity: New challenges, new solutions.* Alexandria, VA: ASCD.

Data Quality Campaign. (2009, June). *Leveraging federal funding for longitudinal data systems: A roadmap for states.* Austin, TX: Author.

Downey, C.J., Steffy, B.E., English, F.W., Frase, L.E., & Poston Jr., W.K. (2004). *The three-minute classroom walk-through: Changing school supervisory practice one teacher at a time.* Thousand Oaks, CA: Corwin Press.

DuFour, R. & Eaker, R. (1998). *Professional learning communities at work: Best practices for enhancing student achievement.* Bloomington, IN: Solution Tree.

Easton, L.B. (Ed.). (2008). *Powerful designs for professional learning* (2nd ed.). Oxford, OH: NSDC.

Epstein, J. (2005). *Developing and sustaining research-based programs of school, family, and community partnerships: Summary of five years of NNPS research.* Baltimore: Johns Hopkins University, Center on School, Family, and Community Partnerships.

Fullan, M. (2001). *Leading in a culture of change.* San Francisco: Jossey-Bass.

Garmston, R.J. & Wellman, B.M. (1999). *The adaptive school: A sourcebook for developing collaborative groups.* Norwood, MA: Christopher-Gordon.

Gay, G. (2000). *Culturally responsive teaching: Theory, research, and practice.* New York: Teachers College Press.

Glatthorn, A., Boschee, F., & Whitehead, B. (2006). *Curriculum leadership: Development and implementation.* Thousand Oaks, CA: Sage Publications.

Gottfredson, D.C., Marciniak, E., Birdseye, A.T., & Gottfredson, G.D. (1995, January/February). Increasing teacher expectations for student achievement. *Journal of Educational Research, 88*(3), 155-163.

Hall, G. & Hord, S. (2001). *Implementing change: Patterns, principles, and potholes.* Boston: Allyn & Bacon.

Holcomb, E.L. (2009). *Asking the right question: Tools for collaboration and school change* (3rd ed.). Thousand Oaks, CA: Corwin Press.

Jensen, E. (1998). *Introduction to brain-compatible learning.* San Diego, CA: The Brain Store.

Killion, J. & Harrison, C. (2006). *Taking the lead: New roles for teachers and school-based coaches.* Oxford, OH: NSDC.

Lewin, R. & Regine, B. (1999). *The soul at work.* London: Orion Business.

Marzano, R.J. (with Marzano, J.S. & Pickering, D.J.). (2003a). *Classroom management that works: Research-based strategies for every teacher.* Alexandria, VA: ASCD.

Marzano, R.J. (2003b). *What works in schools: Translating research into action.* Alexandria, VA: ASCD.

National Staff Development Council. (2001). *NSDC's standards for staff development.* Oxford, OH: Author.

Newmann, F. & Associates. (1996). *Authentic achievement: Restructuring schools for intellectual quality.* San Francisco: Jossey-Bass.

Nieto, S. (2000). *Affirming diversity: The sociopolitical context of multicultural education.* New York: Longman.

Nonaka, I. & Takeuchi, H. (1995). *The knowledge-creating company.* New York: Oxford University Press.

Patterson, K., Grenny, J., McMillan, R., & Switzler, A. (2002). *Crucial conversations: Tools for talking when stakes are high.* New York: McGraw-Hill.

Schlechty, P.C. (2002). *Working on the work: An action plan for teachers, principals, and superintendents.* San Francisco: Jossey-Bass.

Singleton, G. & Linton, C. (2006). *Courageous conversations about race: A field guide for achieving equity in schools.* Thousand Oaks, CA: Corwin Press.

Smith, R. (2001). *Conscious classroom management: Unlocking the secrets of great teaching.* San Rafael, CA: Conscious Teaching Publications.

Tomlinson, C. (2001). *How to differentiate instruction in mixed-ability classrooms.* Alexandria, VA: ASCD.

Vygotsky, L. (1978). Interaction between learning and development. In *Mind in Society.* (Trans. M. Cole). Cambridge, MA: Harvard University Press.

Wald, P. & Castleberry, M. (Eds.). (2000). *Educators as learners: Creating a professional learning community in your school.* Alexandria, VA: ASCD.

About the author

Michael Murphy, a native of Dallas, Texas, is a national consultant and facilitator in the areas of planning, school improvement, systems thinking, curriculum design, and teaching quality. He also is the director for strategic development at the Salesmanship Club Youth and Family Centers in Dallas, where he provides coaching and leadership for two of the agency's programs: the J. Erik Jonsson Community School, an accredited laboratory school serving 232 inner-city children, 3 years old through 5th grade, and the Institute for Excellence in Urban Education, a collaborative research and professional development initiative designed for the exchange of effective practices, the use of tools and protocols for classroom and school improvement, ongoing coaching and professional learning, and customized consulting services. Murphy has also been an adjunct professor and executive lecturer for the University of North Texas in Denton, Texas, a suburb of Dallas, for 14 years.

Murphy has extensive experience in school improvement and uses his love of teaching and learning to facilitate strategic planning and lead professional development seminars throughout the United States. He has published numerous articles for national journals and co-authored *The School Improvement Planning Manual* (NSDC, 1991).

In addition, Murphy is a contributing author for educational books in the last 15 years, including *The Whole-Faculty Study Groups Fieldbook* (Corwin Press, 2007) and *Powerful Designs for Professional Learning* (NSDC, 2008). Murphy has been an active member of the National Staff Development Council for 20 years and was NSDC's director of programs from 1999 to 2004, working with 40 state and provincial affiliate organizations, developing and managing NSDC networks, coordinating the annual conference, managing and leading the NSDC Academies, and presenting on behalf of NSDC.

Murphy has been a teacher, elementary specialist, principal, assistant superintendent, and interim superintendent. He was the executive director of the Principal Assessment and Action Center, a joint collaborative venture between the Region 10 Educational Service Center, the Dallas Independent School District, and the Dallas Institute for Urban Leadership, and was director of product research and development at Westmark Systems, established to provide the highest quality teacher and administrator professional development through the nationally sanctioned American College of Education.

Murphy is married to a fellow educator. He and his wife, Debby, a national reading consultant, have two children, Megan Murphy Hogue, who is completing her pediatric residency in Dallas, and Kevin Murphy, an elementary special education teacher in a Dallas suburb.